# INTRODUCTION

Welcome to the exciting, challenging, rewarding, and important role of Composition Teacher. This book is meant both to be your companion as you begin to teach composition and to offer you ideas as you organize and teach your own freshman writing course.

Teaching writing--like writing itself--is a complex process--one that is informed by an abundance of research, theory, and pedagogical practice. It is also a process that can be systematically learned, can always be changed and improved, and can be truly rewarding. As a new teacher of writing, your teaching assignment is an exciting opportunity to have a genuinely important effect on someone's life. Through your course, students will have refined their ability to communicate--expressively, informatively, and persuasively. In this way, you can make personal, social, academic, and even financial differences in your students' lives because learning to write better is one of the best investments students make in their own futures. Sometimes, it is an investment that few students truly understand or appreciate until they reflect upon the differences that they are able to make in their own lives because they can write well.

This book synthesizes research and practice in every chapter so that you can see where the recommended pedagogies originated in composition research. By making the research and theory an integral part of the practices in the book, I hope to have made the theory accessible to you. While the assumption behind this book is that the audience knows little composition theory and won't before classes begin, the book summarizes many of the major theories in each particular topic area and in this way can be useful to even a veteran teacher.

My own teaching assistants at The University of Texas at El Paso were the inspiration for this approach. When they first came to teach with me, they knew little about composition research or practice, but were always curious about why we were teaching the way we were. To compensate for their inexperience, I integrated succinct discussions of applicable composition theory into our weekly planning sessions. This worked well for them; I hope that it works well for you too.

Teaching College Writing is divided into three parts, each one devoted to an essential ingredient in the process of teaching writing: Part I, Preparing to Teach, describes the kinds of activities that a teacher needs to complete before ever setting foot in the classroom. It summarizes what you should find out about your class before it meets, how to construct your syllabus, and how to design an effective sequence of writing assignments. Part I concludes with a discussion of different writing requirements besides essays and a short bibliography to point you in new directions.

Part II, Teaching: The Early Days, describes in detail the first four classes of the semester (two weeks of classes). This section recommends some activities for the first days of class that will provide you with a piece of writing you will use to assess your students' abilities. Over the course of these two weeks your students really begin the writing activities which are the cornerstone of your course.

Part III, Teaching: Students Writing Essays, is the real substance of this book and your course. It describes for you how to use prewriting in your classroom; techniques for teaching the essay's "outer shape" and "inner parts," i.e., the organization of essays, paragraphs, and sentences; strategies for teaching and implementing revision and revision workshops in your classroom; and some suggestions for having students edit and proofread their drafts. Last, this section looks toward evaluation and summarizes for you a variety of grading approaches.

This book synthesizes the research and practice of the many people whose names appear in the chapter bibliographies. To their fine and inspiring work, I am indebted.

I thank the folks at Allyn & Bacon for their sincere belief in the importance of writing and its teaching. I especially thank Carol Alper and Allen Workman for keeping the project moving forward.

Last, I am grateful to my friends and colleagues at The University of Texas at El Paso for generously donating their time and expertise to conversations with me and to the reading of this manuscript as it was in revision. I especially thank my friend Jeri Gunn for carefully proofreading the final manuscript. These people have made a substantial difference in the final product.

El Paso, TX                                              M.S.
November, 1994

# PART I: PREPARING TO TEACH

What do you need to do before you begin actively to teach? How do you get from the exciting moment of being notified that you will teach Freshman composition to walking through the door on the first day of class? PART I of this book gives you an overview of the tasks in which you'll engage as you prepare to teach. Among these tasks are the following:

- understanding the make-up of your class,

- selecting and studying your textbook,

- designing your syllabus,

- creating writing assignments, and

- locating additional resources.

# CHAPTER 1:
# PLANNING FOR THE SEMESTER

## UNDERSTANDING YOUR CLASS

If you plan your course ahead of time, your mind will be at ease when you come to teach it; thus, first, you need to do some research about the nature of the class you'll be teaching. In doing this research, your best resource will be the Director of Freshman Composition (or some similar title) or the Chairperson of your Department. Either or both of these people, and any experienced teacher in the department, can give you concrete information about the class you'll teach, about the other classes offered by the department, and about how your course fits into the sequence of English classes that your department offers.

From these resource people find out as much about your course as you can: (1) the location of your classroom, (2) the course's role in the superstructure of your department and institution, (3) the makeup of its students.

## YOUR COURSE: ITS LOCATION

As soon as is feasible, find out where your class will be meeting. Once you know where your class will meet, visit the room and even begin to feel what it will be like to teach there. Besides the people that will eventually fill the room, a number of factors can make a real difference in a room's "climate." For example, knowing the following can help you psyche yourself for the location of your class:

- Are there windows?

- Do the desks move, are they bolted to the floor, or are there moveable tables?

- Are there facilities for projectors (film, slide, overhead, etc)?

- Is the room a bit large or small for the size of class you anticipate?

- Is the classroom at the top of several flights of stairs, or is it in the basement?

Can you imagine how many different combinations of rooms you could begin to put together? And each one would give you a different feeling about your class and your teaching.

## YOUR COURSE: IN THE DEPARTMENT

In addition to locating your class's location on campus, find out how your course fits into the department's curricular structure. Some institutions have only one Freshman English course, others as many as four. Often, a department will have formal descriptions of its freshman writing courses, including descriptions of each course's goals, writing expectations, grading criteria, and sample assignments. Because there is so much paperwork to be distributed to faculty, both new and veteran, sometimes these documents that describe your course don't find their way to you promptly, so you might ask if such materials exist in your department.

You might also want answers to questions like the following:

- Will your course give the students credit towards graduation?

- What other writing courses exist in the department?

- What writing courses are required of students?

- How do students get placed into the Freshman course you are teaching?

- Will you be required to give a final exam? If you are required to give a final, is it a department exam, and is it graded by a department panel, or do you grade your own?
- How much of each student's grade and course success depends on this exam?

- How do you deal with unsuccessful students; i.e., if a diligent student seems destined to fail the course, do you have any recourse such as giving a pass/fail grade instead of a letter grade? Can you withdraw him or her from your course? If so, when is the withdrawal deadline?

• How do you deal with troublesome students?

Answers to these questions--and others like them--will begin to give you a picture of your teaching situation.

## YOUR COURSE: ITS STUDENTS

The students who are placed into your course are the most important ingredient that shape the character of your course. Students are placed into Freshman English courses in a variety of ways: based on their scores on national exams such as the SAT (Scholastic Aptitude Test) or the ACT (American College Test), based on a new Acuplacer computerized placement technique, or based on a specially-designed university placement exam. At any rate, universities across the country have different procedures for placing entering freshman and different cut-off scores on national exams for entrance into standard Freshman English classes. It is useful to know how the students are placed into your course and what that will mean for the abilities that your students will possess.

At most universities, you likely will have a broad range of student ability. In this vein, for example, you might have a class of students who fall into the category of English as a Second Language for students of Basic Writing, students who are getting their skills up to par before the "real" freshman English class. On the other hand, you might have a special section of "honors" students. You can, however, assume that you'll have regular Freshman students unless you've been told otherwise. In any case, you should find out about adjunct support services that exist for students. Most campuses now have tutorial services for students. These services generally include a specific place or service for writing assistance where peers are trained to assist students in writing and revising their papers for English classes. You can also make special arrangements with some writing centers whereby you send the students to the writing facility, and the tutors there will look for specific features in the students' responses to your assignment. This gives students additional reader response for their essays, at the same time that it makes the students feel more comfortable about going to the writing center in the future.

Last, find out the particulars about your specific class: the number of credit hours the course carries, how large the class will be, what time of day it meets. Since freshman writing classes can carry anywhere from 3 to 6 credit hours, find out how many credit hours students will earn by taking the class you'll teach.  The number of hours has a direct bearing on how much work students will be able to and be willing to complete during the semester.  Classes may meet at different times and on different days, so this is an important piece of information to know.  For a three-credit-hour course (the most standard of the credit-hour options), a course might meet for three 50-minute sessions, two 1-hour-and-20 minute sessions, or one 2-hour-and-50-minute session.  Thus, individual class period length also has a bearing on how much work you can get done during a particular class period and the kinds of activities you can plan.

## CHOOSING YOUR BOOK

When it comes to choosing a book, you will find one of 2 possibilities exist.  Either your department prescribes a text or texts for your use or you get to choose your own.  Either option has its strengths.

## DEPARTMENT SELECTION

If your department has selected texts, you often still get a choice.  Department committees often select a range of texts that they recommend for use in a particular writing class.  Then, you can choose yours from among these.  If the department has selected a particular text (or texts) for your use, you will have to develop a teaching style that is consonant with the texts that they have chosen.  If you have not taught before, having a department-selected text can be a blessing because it immediately eliminates lots of alternatives--known and unknown.  This option eliminates looking for your own textbook, a very time-consuming activity.  Also, if the department chooses the text for you, it means that some teaching veterans will be using, and have used before, the same text so you will find plentiful teaching materials that have been used previously and been successful.  Even so, you should study the book or books that you are going to use very carefully so that you can understand the philosophy behind the course you will teach.  Some books progress according to aims and purposes for writing, from personal essays to informative essays to persuasive essays, while other texts are organized according to rhetorical modes (narration, description, and so on).  Some texts are organized around academic disciplines, some according to themes; others are organized as writing process, collaborative writing texts.  Each of these organizational patterns represents a philosophy for teaching composition that you might want to investigate more fully if you have not studied composition as a scholarly discipline.

## INSTRUCTOR SELECTION

If the department does not select composition texts for its faculty, you will need to select your own textbook. If so, you must think about what is important to you in the teaching and writing process. If you have never taught writing, you might know intuitively that there are a distinct number of choices for the overall organization of your course: rhetorical modes approach (e.g., description, comparison and contrast, definition, etc.); the aims and purposes approach (e.g., expressive, informative, persuasive); a thematic approach (e.g., family crises, university policies, community programs). Your book choice will reflect a teaching philosophy that you will teach for at least a semester, so choose textbooks cautiously. Often people choose more than one text: a handbook and a reader, for example. In this way, you have one text that works students through the essay writing process accompanied by another text that is used as a resource for surface features (grammar, punctuation, sentence construction, et cetera). In the case of a reader, you can use these essays as examples to demonstrate essay development, paragraph structure, word choice, punctuation variation, introductions, conclusions, style, and so on.

Book selection can be aided by a number of sources: your colleagues--experienced teaching assistants, full-time faculty, and part-time faculty--will have copies of texts; publishers who will offer examination copies for instructors to review; both the university and your department libraries will have copies of textbooks from recent use.

## DESIGNING THE SYLLABUS

Once you understand what the make-up of your class will be and know what your textbook will be, you are ready to design your syllabus. The syllabus actually is considered a binding agreement by most institutions, so this is the place to establish your rules and regulations as well as to identify your basic assignments and grade distribution.

Often a department will require you to submit copies of your syllabus to its office. This can be used as supporting material if questions about the content of your course arise. Also, when classes begin, students examine your syllabus to determine what your course will be like when they are "shopping around" for the right course. So the syllabus has more far-reaching uses than it might at first glance appear to have. As Erika Lindemann (1987) points out in her indispensable book for writing teachers, "Because the syllabus serves not only as information but also as a teaching tool, it should be designed carefully and revised frequently, each term incorporating improvements based on previous experiences with the course" (23).

When you envision your course, especially with a writing course, it is often difficult to decide what topics should come first. Unfortunately, a writing course isn't like a math course where the content is cumulative. In a writing course, it seems as if students need to know everything all at once if they are going to write an essay, so you have to decide among the options. A whole course (besides the sequencing of major assignments we'll talk more about in the next chapter) can progress from, as William Irmscher says, the whole to its parts or the parts to the whole (63). If the course moves from the whole to its parts, you assume that your students are able to piece together a composition already. You continue by focusing, over the course of the semester, on organization, paragraphing, sentence structure, and the surface features of spelling, punctuation, word choice. Alternatively, if you choose the second approach and move from part to whole, you move from words to sentences and paragraphs and finally to essays. The first approach actually is more in synch with the writing process which assumes that a writer gets ideas, puts them on paper, then works to organize those ideas, and last, manipulates style and mechanics. You will need to decide which sequence suits your style better because if you are comfortable with the sequence, the students will be also.

Checklist for Designing Your Course Syllabus "Checklist for Designing Your Course Syllabus". The following "Checklist for Designing Your Course Syllabus" was adapted from the recommendations made by Lindemann in her book, A Rhetoric for Writing Teachers.

1. "Nitty-gritty" of the course

• Semester date (e.g., Fall 199_)

• Call number and complete title for the course

• Course meeting times and location

- Your name, office location, office phone number, office hours

- Text books and other materials to be purchased--include complete bibliographic information for texts
- A brief description of the course--adapted from the catalog and indicating your own emphasis

2. Course policies and procedures

- Attendance policies--many instructors, even departments, feel that it is essential for students to be in class, so instructors set fairly strict attendance policies.

- Revision policies--state clearly how you will handle revision of papers, how many revisions are permissible, when they must be turned in, and how they will be evaluated.

- Due dates--state very plainly your policy regarding the date when any textbook or supplemental homework assignments or major papers are due. If you will accept late work, spell out the conditions that are acceptable (and NOT acceptable) to you.

- Plagiarism--Good to make a statement about this in your own syllabus even though it's probably in your college catalog.

- Goals of the course--explain what your goals for the course are, what the purpose of the course is, and what the course will prepare students to do (e.g., "This course prepares you to address a variety of audiences and purposes in your writing.")

- Physical preparation of students' papers--describe exactly what you expect drafts to look like (e.g., "Both your rough draft for peer review in class and your final draft must be word processed or typed.") and what you want turned in with the finished product (e.g., "Clip together your self-evaluation, your audience analysis, your two peer-review forms, your rough draft, and your final draft.").

3. Description of Assignments

- Formal assignments--describe as clearly and completely as you can what the major papers will entail (length, topic, etc).

- Informal assignments--since some assignments (textbook homework, journal entries, in-class work, etc) will be decidedly different from the students' formal written assignments for your course, acknowledge how much of the grade these will occupy, how they will be graded, and generally what you expect of each.

4. Grading

- Course requirements--what MUST a student complete minimally to pass your course (e.g., "To PASS the course: You must complete the journal, the four major papers, and receive a passing grade on 2 of the 3 'on-the-spot' writings . . . .")

- Formal written work--How will the major papers be weighted? What percentage of the final course grade does each major paper receive? Often, the first paper will be worth less (e.g., maybe 10%) than later papers (e.g., 15%, then 20%, and so on).

- Informal work--Describe how much of the grade other work will occupy. For example, if you have students keep a journal, how much is it worth towards the final grade? How will you credit the peer review process and homework from their textbooks?

5. Calendar of daily assignments

- Provide a day-by-day calendar of assignments, complete with page numbers from the text and/or information about the papers that will be due (e.g., dates for rough drafts, peer review sessions, final drafts, revised drafts, etc.).

6. Class meetings

- Since college writing classes are often conducted in a workshop fashion, and since this is very different from the other classes that most students have probably taken, it is a good idea to describe this on your syllabus. Describe how much time will be devoted to in-class workshops, in-class writing, student presentations, and lectures.

Sample Syllabus. The following syllabus is a sample of the kinds of assignments and policies you might establish. Most importantly, remember that you should keep your syllabus somewhat open so that you can make changes in it as you move through the semester. Regard it as a loose plan for what you hope to accomplish during the semester.

---

September 19__

TO:              Freshman Composition Students
FROM:            Your Instructor
SUBJECT:         Course syllabus and policies

I. Where, when, and how to find me:
    Office:
    Office hours:
    Office phone:


II. What you will need:

    Full bibliographic information for your textbook(s)
    A dictionary
    A pocket folder in which to submit all of your work, and
    A LIGHTWEIGHT loose-leaf notebook.


III. General Policies and Procedures

1.    Get to know one another quickly, since this course is conducted collaboratively, with primary teaching responsibilities shared by everyone. Exchange phone numbers with two or three people from the class, and get assignments from them on the days that you must miss class.

2.    Attendance is important and rewarded.  If you miss 4 or more classes, you will be dropped from the course if this occurs before the drop deadline; otherwise, you'll receive an "F" for the course.  Also please arrive punctually and plan to stay for the entire class.  This policy includes attending scheduled conferences -- missing a conference is an absence.

3.    All major papers are to be typewritten or word processed.  This includes drafts brought in for workshop purposes.  Other work (notebook entries, freewriting, showing writing, etc) may be handwritten on lined paper.

4.    Late work is not acceptable.  Hand your work in on time and be prepared to speak on assigned dates.  Work not turned in at class time on the designated date will not receive credit.  This includes rough drafts and textbook assignments, as well as the drafts.

5.    Please save all of your work in your notebook so that we can see your progress throughout the semester and at the end of the semester.  This includes (1) your journal, (2) your essays and rough drafts, and (3) workshopping and other in-class writing.

6.    You will incur some costs during the semester.  You will also incur an occasional photocopying cost during the semester.  However, if you use the computers to prepare your assignments, you can order additional printouts.

7.    The use of another person's work as your own of could result in a grade of "F" for the course and a visit with the Dean.

8.    To pass the course you must complete the journal, the 4 major papers, and receive a passing grade on 2 of the 3 "on-the-spot" writings.

Submitting your essays: Submit your each essay in the pocket folder that I asked you to purchase.  Place the finished essay on one side of the folder with the self-evaluation clipped to the top of it.  On the other side of the folder, clip together, your prewriting, your rough draft, and the comments that you wrote about other people's work.

IV.    GRADING
Your final grade for the course will be determined in the following way:
        Essays                          80 %
        Notebook                        10 %
        (includes journal entries, showing writing, and other in-class
        writing activities)
        Workshop activities             10%

---

## CALENDAR

        The following calendar details your assignments for the
semester. As we begin each new writing assignment, I will give you a
new handout specifying the exact nature of the assignment--the
audience, your purpose for writing, a calendar of additional writing
activities, etc. Plan the reading assignments in the text you have chosen
to correlate with the coursework.

| WEEK | IN-CLASS WORK | ASSIGNMENT |
|---|---|---|
| 1 | Introduction to the course: syllabus, policies. | Read:  (assigned reading) |
|  | In-class essay. | Write: Begin your journal. |
|  | Introductions of each other to the class. | Assignment # 1: Expressive writing.  We'll talk about the rhetorical context for this assignment--its purpose and its audience. |
|  | Introduction to journal keeping (Freewriting, etc.). |  |

| | | |
|---|---|---|
| 2 | Introduction to prewriting techniques and "showing writing." | Read: (assigned reading) |
| | | Write: Practice invention techniques in your journal. |
| | Surveying your field for topics or ideas to write about. | Complete daily "showing writing" paragraphs. |
| | Introduction to working with other students | |
| 3 | Introduction to peer review techniques. | Read: (assigned reading) |
| | | Rough draft workshop in class. |
| | Have individual conferences either in the classroom or in my office. | On the day of the workshop,bring 3 typed copies. |
| | | Sign up for conferences with your instructor. |
| 4 | Timed writing--answering exam questions. | Read: (assigned reading) |
| | | Write: Continue "showing writing" practice. |
| | Preparing manuscripts for handing in. | |
| | | Essay #1 due next time. Complete the self-evaluation after your essay is finished. See instructions above for handing in your essay. |

| 5 | Essay # 1 due. | Read: (assigned reading) |
|---|---|---|
| | First "on-the-spot" writing. | Assignment # 2: Informative writing. Once again, I'll provide you with a handout that details the assignment and we'll talk in class about the rhetorical context for this assignment. We'll also look at 2 sample essays. |
| | More about writing effective sentences. | |
| | | Continue daily showing writing practice. |
| 6 | Building paragraphs. | Read: (assigned reading) |
| | | Write: Invention practice for second essay. Continue freewriting and sharing ideas. |
| 7 | Writing sentences with variety and concise sentences. | Read: (assigned reading) |
| 8 | Diction: Using appropriate words. | Rough draft workshop in class. |
| | | On the day of the workshop, bring 3 typed copies. |
| | Have individual conferences either in the classroom or in my office. | Sign up for conferences with your instructor. |
| 9 | Revision | Essay #2 due next time. After you have completed your essay, complete the self-evaluation. |
| | | On-the-spot #2 next time. |

| | | |
|---|---|---|
| 10 | Essay #2 is due.<br><br>On-the-spot #2.<br><br>Choosing effective words. | Assignment # 3: Informative/persuasive writing. I'll provide you with a handout that details the assignment and we'll talk in class about the rhetorical context for this assignment. We'll also look at 2 sample essays.<br><br>Read: (assigned reading)<br><br>Write: More freewriting, invention, and showing writing. |
| 11 | Using figurative language. | Read: (assigned reading)<br><br>Rough draft workshop in class.<br><br>On the day of the workshop, bring 3 typed copies.<br><br>Sign up for conferences with your instructor. |
| 12 | Essay #3 due.<br><br>On-the-spot # 3.<br><br>The persuasive essay and fallacies in reasoning. | Assignment # 4: Persuasive writing. I'll provide you with a handout that details the assignment and we'll talk in class about the rhetorical context for this assignment. We'll also look at 2 sample essays.<br><br>Read: (assigned reading)<br><br>Write: More invention, freewriting, and showing writing. |

| 13 | Inductive and deductive reasoning | Read: (assigned reading)<br><br>Select a topic for your essay, thinking about the opposition that exists and how you might counter that. |
|----|----|----|
| 14 | Share your arguments for sound reasoning and opposing arguments. | Rough draft workshop in class.<br><br>On the day of the workshop, bring 3 typed copies.<br><br>Sign up for conferences with your instructor. |
| 15 | Essay # 4 due.<br><br>Presentation of final paper to the class.<br><br>Course wrap-up and evaluations. | Select one of the first three essays to revise and submit with your complete notebook. |

At your final exam time, I'll expect you to turn in your complete notebook from English 3111. Be sure that your notebook is well organized and neat--remember to number and date all of your entries. Place your revised essay in the front of your notebook.

## MAKING LESSON PLANS

Lesson plans are an elaboration of your syllabus, but they are written for your eyes, not the students'. More importantly, lesson plans help you organize your time and materials efficiently and effectively. In your lesson plans, itemizing the following will help you to conceptualize a given class period:

- what the students will have completed by classtime,
- your teaching objectives for that day,
- what activities will take place in class that day, and

- the class minutes portioned into the activities you wish to complete.

Lesson plans are often in the form of an informal outline with notes to yourself about the points you want to be certain to make and the way that you'll make those points. It is almost necessary to make lesson plans week by week for a writing class. If you make them too far in advance, you don't leave room to revise them according to the needs of your students.

---

Example
Day 2 -- Sample Lesson Plan

Each student will have
- read the assigned reading  introducing the purposes for writing
- made descriptive notes about a person in preparation to write a descriptive paragraph

My objectives for the class are to have students
- get a feel for writing for different purposes
- introduce students to "showing writing." This will be the beginning of their attention to detail in all of their writing.

The activities we will complete and the time they'll take
- 15 minutes--discuss the text
  What do you remember from the introduction?
  What is the writing process?
  How do different situations call for different kinds of writing?
  What do you know now that you didn't know before you read for class?

- 30 minutes--introduce "showing writing" by doing the following:
  1. Have students pretend that they are sitting in a park. They look up and see a frisky, shaggy dog romping in the park.
  2. Have students write a paragraph describing it.
  3. Walk around and look at what students are writing. Put an "X" by any sentence that gives good details about the scene.
  4. Write FRISKY SHAGGY DOG on the board
  5. Have students com up with words or phrases that first describe DOG, then SHAGGY, then FRISKY.

6. Ask them to look at their own: Did they come up with these details in their paragraphs?
7. Have students read the sentences that you put an "X" beside.
8. Have them use the notes they brought to class with them to write a descriptive paragraph about someone using the sentence, "The person I am describing is X." The "X" is a characteristic that they fill in, but cannot use in their paragraph. If they don't finish, they can take it home to finish.

---

One caution about your lesson plans: Sometimes they need to be revised on the spot because an activity takes more or less time than you had anticipated. In writing classes, enthusiasm is important, so if your students are engaged in a discussion of the text, for example, let the discussion continue a few minutes longer than you had scheduled. You can make up the time on another activity--such as the in-class portion of a writing project, which can be taken home to finish.

While you need to be well prepared, even over prepared, you should also be flexible. The key to a successful class is to be able to change directions and omit something or add something during the course of a period.

WORKS CITED Chapter 1

Irmscher, William F. Teaching Expository Writing. New York: Holt, Rinehart and Winston, 1979.
Lindemann, Erika. A Rhetoric for Writing Teachers. New York: Oxford University Press, 1987.

# CHAPTER 2:
# CREATING WRITING ASSIGNMENTS

Creating good writing assignments, ones that are intellectually stimulating, manageable, and clear is a skill. We now know, thanks to Lindemann, Moffett, Kinneavy, and others that assignments ought to follow a particular sequence and that they also should address a particular audience for a specific purpose.

This chapter discusses how to sequence writing assignments and how to recognize more complex writing problems. This chapter also discusses composing activities that can be undertaken within a single assignment, as well as the kinds of writing besides essays with which your students can and should have some experience.

## CREATING THE SEQUENCE OF ASSIGNMENTS

The course that you teach and the writing that students produce for you are only as good as the assignments that you prepare. Assignments that generate quality student thought and are a pleasure to read are rarely, if ever, dashed off at the beginning of class, given orally, or scribbled hurriedly on the board. They are, instead, placed in a sequence of other assignments, have a specific purpose in the grand scheme of the course, and are interesting to students.

To respond to this challenge, think about your whole course before it begins, not in specific detail, but in overall terms. How do you want your series of major assignments to proceed? How does one piece lead to another? How does each one fit naturally in the sequence of events?

A writing assignment should be more than something a student responds to in writing and that a teacher judges. According to Richard L. Larson, "Its purpose should be to teach, to give students an experience in composing (selecting, arranging, and expressing thoughts) from which he can learn as much as he can. . . . The very act of writing the assignment should help the student think a little more incisively, reason a little more soundly, and write a little more effectively than he did before encountering it" (209).

Writing assignments should not be designed in isolation from the rest of the course. Rather, they should be placed in a particular sequence to allow the student to build on what he or she has already learned about writing. To accomplish this, a series of effective writing assignments should ask students to address progressively more complex rhetorical problems, dealing with increasingly more complex relationships between the writer, her subject, and her audience. By varying the demands of our assignments, we give students practice in adjusting these relationships (Lindemann, 193).

## THE WRITER'S AIM

This book helps you to place student essays in a sound sequence by recommending that your assignments move over the course of the semester according to an overall aim (or purpose) for writing. This means that you will have your students begin with expressive essays, move to informative ones, and probably conclude with persuasive writing. This progression adheres to the advice of contemporary rhetorician, James L. Kinneavy, who maintains that when we create writing assignments this sequence provides students with increasingly complex writing problems.

As far back as Aristotle, classical rhetoricians knew that all discourse was the product of its relationship among three factors--the subject itself, the writer, and the reader or audience  These three factors form what is commonly called the communication triangle. Interestingly, a piece of discourse could address any of the three relationships of the triangle--from the simplest to the most complex.

For example, an expressive writing assignment focuses on the writer (your student) and that student's experience of the subject (usually a personal experience).   Since the source of the information for expressive writing is generally within the writer, it is usually considered the least demanding writing task.  An informative writing assignment, in contrast, asks the student to move beyond him or herself to focus more on the subject itself, relating information about the subject to the audience.  And, last, persuasive writing focuses least on the writer, most on the audience.  A persuasive aim in writing is the most difficult to master.  The aim of persuasive writing is to convince the audience to think or act or believe as the writer does.  To accomplish this, the writer must focus most on the audience's experience of the subject rather than the writer's own.   In other words, if a student believes that the university's registration procedures are outdated, he will almost naturally assume that the university need only be told about this for them to go about fixing the problem.  The student doesn't immediately step into the university's shoes and view all the possible problems that there are to solve before they can decide where to spend the available money.  Through persuasive writing, the students will learn how to step out of their own perspective and view situations from another point of view.

Nearly any subject can be used as evidence to address all of these aims, depending upon the focus that the writer chooses. For example, a student might choose to write expressively about his/her experience of Yosemite National Park. In doing this, the student would write using his senses as a guide, and, subsequently, the reader would get the writer's impressions of Yosemite. If on the next assignment, the student chose to write about hiking in national parks, he could draw on his experience of Yosemite as he informs his readers about how to hike the national forest. Last, the student may be an environmentalist who seeks to convince the public that national forests are in danger of extinction because of the general public's abuse of these natural resources. In this essay, his aim is to persuade the reader to take action. In each of these essays, the writer is choosing to shift the relationships among subject, writer, and audience to serve the aims of the essay, and thus he takes on an increasingly more complex writing task.


THE WRITER'S ROLE

A writing assignment should encourage a student to take on a specific role as the writer. Erika Lindemann says that we "should encourage role-playing because it allows students to imagine rhetorical situations and audiences outside academic contexts" (194).

Using the vehicle of the writing assignment, a student comes to understand that she possesses a myriad of possible voices, that she can speak and write from a variety of roles as a Freshman Composition student. For example, often times a student will not realize that her personal ethos includes that of a daughter, a "best friend," and an employee (which alone includes a vertical and horizontal business-type roles), a former student, a person who holds opinions and can communicate those and have them printed in the newspaper, a member of community and university organizations--just to name a few of the potential roles an eighteen year old student could possess. A student will come up with an amazing array of differences if she is asked, "When you describe your Friday night date, do you write and speak to your mother differently from the manner in which you address your best friend? What do you vary?"

## THE WRITER'S TASK: SOME GUIDELINES

With all of the information that is available to consider, what are the basics of making a good writing assignment? Consider the following questions as you design your writing assignments. They represent a synthesis of what Lindemann (194) and Larson (Training, 109-110) recommend:

1. Why have you chosen this assignment? Make it clear how this assignment fits into the sequence of writing assignments in the course.

2. Will the assignment engage your students' interest?

3. Will the assignment challenge your students to engage in some original thinking?

4. Can this assignment be completed successfully by students who are writing at different levels?

5. Is the task clearly defined for the students? They should have a clear idea of what their paper is meant to accomplish. If you have a model response in the back of your mind, let them know what it is.

6. Have you described a viable audience or choice of audiences to whom the students will write?

7. Are both the role that students are asked to inhabit as writers and the overall writing situation credible?

8. What will the students need to know to perform successfully on the assignment? Conversely, what will you have to teach if you are to assume that students can do well on the assignment?

The above questions will help you to consider the construction of your writing assignments. One last piece of advice: don't withhold information from your students. When you distribute the assignment (YES! It should be carefully written out for them), explain it fully from your point of view, allowing for questions. If you know where students can trip up, you might want to point that out to them. Also, explain to

them how you will read and evaluate their papers: what you will look at
as you evaluate their final drafts (Larson, Teaching, 216-218).

## THE WRITER'S TOPIC

When you create writing assignments, one of the most
important decisions you make is choosing the topic or subject matter
focus for the assignment.    While students want and deserve some
freedom in topic selection, too much choice can lead to floundering.  If
we consider this fact, then what makes a good topic for writing
assignments?    The following recommendations are based on what
Irmscher (69) recommends.  A good topic takes the following into
account:

1.  An aim or purpose that goes beyond the course--i.e., beyond
    just producing a written product;

2.  Concrete situations that engage the students' interest and are
    meaningful within the student's own experience, rather than
    abstract ones;

3.  A stimulus and focus for the student's thinking, actually
    encouraging even the most reticent of writers to write, but
    leaving room for the student to write about experiences and
    issues that s/he has something to write about;

4.  An audience beyond the teacher--even though the teacher is
    always in the backs of students' minds, you can help them think
    past yourself as the teacher-examiner;

5.  A role for the student to inhabit as s/he writes--taking roles as
    student writers is important as they develop as writers and need
    to address both academic and nonacademic audiences; and

6.  A form for the piece of writing (essay, letter, etc.).

As the teacher, you want to arrange the rhetorical structure of
the parts of your course "in a sequence which is cumulative in the sense
that each new structure tends to include those preceding it, so that when
a student learns to handle one kind of structure, he can use that
experience to master the next kind" (McCrimmon, 225).  Thus, it is your
task to design a progression of writing assignments that do this for the

student.  If you ask your students to write a persuasive essay before they have practiced describing their experiences, they are more likely to experience frustration than if you build up to persuasive writing tasks. Students should build gradually on what they are learning.

A last word about sequencing assignments brings me to talk about two issues: selecting the audience for the piece and sequencing within the assignment itself.


SELECTING THE AUDIENCE

James Moffett, in The Universe of Discourse, maintains that the superstructure of all discourse is the set of relations among the speaker, the listener, and the subject.  Variations in discourse, he says, occur by altering the time and space between the speaker (writer) and the listener (audience).

In elaborating this theory, Moffett recommends that students be given audiences to write to that gradually move the students over a space and time continuum: away from themselves as audiences (closest in space) and the present (what is now happening).  This provides students with an increasingly complex audience to address.  Thus, students might actually be asked to write for themselves initially.  If this kind of writing assignment seems difficult to conceptualize, consult Moffett who recommends that we ask them to write diary or journal entries as a first writing assignment.  Then, moving away from themselves and focusing on the rhetorical choices of the communication triangle, they can write about the same issue in dialogue,  increasing the complexity of their audience to a face-to-face relationship.  Next, Moffett recommends that students move to increasingly more public audiences, ultimately writing for an audience they do not know and about theory and speculation.  A progression such as this takes students through a continuum of space and time as they consider their audiences.

Practically speaking, what does this continuum of space and time mean?  Time, in Moffett's scheme, is related to verb tense--present, past, and future--while space identifies how close to the audience the writer is.  Moffett establishes the time-space sequence to look something like ththe illustration below  (35-47).

This continuum of time and space reflects the movement from strictly private to wholly public audiences with which our students should have practice.

| What is happening | interior dialogue<br>conversation<br>personal journal |
|---|---|
| What happened | correspondence<br>autobiography<br>memoir |
| What happens if . . . | History<br>(Generalizing from what<br>we know) |
| What may happen if . . . | Scientific writing<br>(Theorizing, arguing,<br>speculating about what<br>might or could come<br>about based on what we<br>know) |

## SEQUENCING WITHIN A SINGLE ASSIGNMENT

Within any given major writing assignments, have students practice the full range of writing activities: prewriting, writing, revising, and publishing (e.g., to a small group in the class, the whole class, and/or the teacher). Each of these stages to the writing process is discussed in more detail both in future chapters of this book and, most likely, in the textbook you re using.

Prewriting activities, such as those that are coming up in Chapter 6, give students the opportunity, if they need it, to discover what it is they have to say.

Next, students can begin to draft the body of their essay trying out different organizational patterns, using a variety of details, adding and deleting material as they move back and forth through the body of their essay. This stage is often brought to fruition when students read one another's work and make recommendations for altering or maintaining the content and organization. Sometimes this students-reading-students stage is repeated. Students may suggest revisions and reread one another's work, eventually making simple editorial recommendations to polish up a nearly finished piece.

Last, students publish their work by turning it over to the teacher for reading. This stage may also be repeated. Since revision is such an important part of the writing process, a teacher might read the essay, recommend revisions, talk with the student, and return the essay ungraded, after which the student revises and submits a final essay, this time for grading.

## THE ASSIGNMENT PACKET

For me, a completed assignment packet includes the following items:

- a handout describing the assignment,

- a calendar of reading and writing assignments to prepare the students for writing the paper,

- two peer-critique forms to guide students' reading of one another's papers, and

- a scoring guide.

What follows is a sample assignment for the first essay of four in a semester. This one is essentially an expressive essay assignment.

---

Finding Meaning in Your Experience

The essay that you are going to write asks you to remember an important person, place, or event from your life.

Imagine that the your university's weekly newspaper is sponsoring a contest for the best essay written by a freshman that is based on his/her own experience. The readers of this newspaper (and so of your essay) are campus employees and students your own age with your same interests. With this scenario in mind, write an essay in which you recreate an important point in your life and relate the meaning of this experience. Consider one of the following:

1. Describe a brief incident in your life that changed you in some important way. Show this incident so that your readers can vividly experience it through your words and understand what and how you learned from it.

2. Describe a phase in your life that changed you in some significant way, a phase or a time when everything seemed to come together or fall apart. Describe this phase vividly and relate the significance of the change. Make your reader "see" what was happening to you and understand why this phase was so important to you.

3. Select a significant person in your life. Describe this person and show how s/he was significant to you. You may use characterization and anecdote as well as "showing" descriptions to help your reader "see" this person.

Write about your personal experience in a way that is so true and well detailed that your reader will live through it with you. Remember to "show" with vivid detail in order for your experience to come to life. You must include what this experience means to you, what you learned from it, or how it changed you. Think of the experience and the meaning as being linked together. You can't have one without the other. It should be about 500-600 words (2-3 typed, double-spaced pages).

| Typed first draft & 3 copies | due _____ |
| Typed final draft | due _____ |

---

## BESIDES MAJOR PAPERS

The kinds of major essays that I've been talking about form only part of your course. There are other kinds of writing activities with which students should have some practice. These include assessment writing, timed (on-the-spot) writing, and journal writing.

### ASSESSMENT WRITING

Assessment (sometimes called diagnostic) writing is a sample of students' writing that you solicit as early as possible in the semester; it is used to assess the strengths and weaknesses that exist in individual students' writing and in your class as a whole. An in-class essay is sufficient for this. Often, I ask students to write a letter introducing themselves to me and telling me anything they think I need to know. I also ask them to identify what they think the course will be like or what they hope to gain from the course (more about this in Chapter 4).

When assessment writing is returned to students it can be accompanied by comments, a scoring guide, and some direction to get the student started. On the other hand, some instructors keep the diagnostic piece for their records. Generally, it is not marked up and graded, though.

The scoring guide on the next page directs the student to specific areas where he or she needs to review.


## TIMED ("ON-THE-SPOT") WRITING

Timed "On-the-spot" writing is an in-class essay. Writing of this sort prepares students for the many essay exams they'll take during their academic careers. If we are preparing our students for their academic careers, practicing with the essay format during a pressure situation is an important part of our mission. Students will experience many situations when they do not have the time to engage in the whole writing process, nor do they want or need to, so it is our job to prepare them for these writing occasions too.

Generally, to prepare students for an "on-the-spot" writing, I give them an essay to read that is accompanied by some thought provoking questions that link the essay to their own lives. In class, I ask them to respond to one of those questions or to a new one that is similar. As a rule, I grade these essays on a holistic pass/fail basis, using a scoring guide such as the following.

A scoring guide to accompany timed (on-the-spot) writing follows the one for assessment writing.

Assessment of _____'s Writing

    Based on this sample of your writing, you may have the following strengths and weaknesses in your writing. Those items needing work are marked "NW" while those that are especially well done are marked "WD." Those items that are not marked are just fine for someone who is about to take a Freshman Composition course.

_____ The writing clearly takes the audience into account.
_____ The writing has an engaging persona/voice.
_____ The writing is clear and direct.
_____ The writing is thoughtful.
_____ The writing has a clear focus.
_____ The ideas in the writing are easy to follow.
_____ The introduction gets the reader's attention, or sets up what is to follow.
_____ Conclusion summarizes or leaves the reader with something to think about.
_____ There are no unnecessary sentences.
_____ Plenty of elaboration, details, examples.
_____ Paragraphing is well done.
_____ Spelling has been carefully checked.
_____ Typing/hand writing is neat, producing a nice looking paper.

    Your editing skills are weak in the areas checked below. Please locate the section in your textbook or in your handbook that explains these skills for some review.

_____ Paragraphing
_____ Clear sentences
_____ Appropriate word choice
_____ Fragments and run-ons
_____ Pronoun agreement & reference
_____ Verb tense, mood, voice
_____ Non-standard forms
_____ Commas, apostrophe
_____ Other punctuation marks
_____ Capitals, homonyms
_____ Abbreviations, numbers, underlining

_____ 's  "On-the-Spot"  Writing

Though it is only one aspect of your writing ability, writing in timed situations is a necessary writing skill.

_____    This "on-the-spot" writing is passing!

_____    This "on-the-spot" writing is not passing for the reasons cited below.

The essay did not pass because of one or more of the following:

_____    The essay did not meet the demands of the assignment

_____    The essay is not focused

_____    Paragraphs contained unrelated sentences, i.e., they contained more than one idea.

_____    Sentences were difficult to understand.

_____    The essay had many editorial errors in spelling, sentence construction (run-ons, fragments, comma splices), capitalization, punctuation, and so on.

Additional comments:

What to do next:

## JOURNAL (INFORMAL) WRITING

Journal and other kinds of informal writing have become an extraordinarily widely used and valuable kind of writing both in Freshman Composition classes and in classes in content courses. For that reason, I'll spend some time describing the nature of journal writing and some of the potential uses for it as a learning tool in your classes.

Often an instructor will ask students to write in a journal (also referred to as a log, a notebook, etc.). Whatever it is called by the instructor, the journal has similar goals for both the students and the professor. This kind of informal writing is called WRITING TO LEARN. This may seem like odd terminology since students assume that all writing is for learning. But in fact, some writing is for the students' own ends and this is writing to learn; other kinds of writing are for the professor's benefit, to show him or her that the student has, in fact, learned. This description of journal writing explains the differences and elaborates on how and why journal writing (or informal kinds of writing) is used in a class.

Writing to learn is different from writing that shows learning in several important ways. First, it involves students with learning in an active rather than a passive role. By asking students to use writing as a tool for learning, you are urging them to interact with the information that they have heard in class and have read for class. Then, they are also asked to speculate on and explore their own ideas as they make sense of the information that they are taking in.

Second, writing to learn puts the emphasis on understanding and applying what they, as students, are learning, not on the mechanics of that product.

Third, writing to learn enables students to interact with the material from their classes on an ongoing basis rather than all at once, in a "one shot" study or writing session. The end product of writing to learn is original thinking--students who are thinking and making connections among ideas for themselves. Following are some suggestions for implementing this kind of writing in your classes.

Using a writing/reading journal gives students a particular place to accumulate writing-to-learn activities. In this journal, students complete any one of a variety of activities that you have asked them to complete. The activities for the journal can vary in degrees of informality and in the tightness of their forms. Journal writing can be used to structure the class and to give students opportunities to interact with the class material. Use journal writing in one of the following ways:

1. <u>To Begin Class</u>.  To bridge previous activities and to get students thinking about a particular class, you might ask them to write for five minutes at the beginning of class time.  There are several ways that you can initiate writing to begin class:

- By giving an "idea prompt" that is related to the day's discussion;
- By providing a quote from the reading for the day and asking students to respond to it;
- By posing a question that will focus students' attention on the day's class.

After allowing five minutes (or so) for responding freely to this prompt, you might ask a student to read his/her response to initiate discussion.  These writing activities work well to bridge students' other activities, such as a previous class or a visit to the Union, and to set the mood for English class.

2. <u>As Transitions in Class</u>.  Informal writing is also useful as a means to focus students' attention during the class.  For example, you could interrupt the discussion and, midstream through the class, ask students to write for five minutes about a particularly hard concept or controversial notion.  This strategy works especially well if there is confusion about a particular point.  Writing down thoughts often helps students to sort out the difficult portions and to make sense of concepts that are confusing and complex.  Then students have the opportunity to interact with the material while the stimulus is still fresh.

3. <u>End Class</u>.  Informal writing can also be used to close class sessions; you could pose a summarizing question, such as, "What one thing did you learn today?"  This kind of question asks students to synthesize the material for themselves.

4. <u>Outside Classtime</u>.  Informal writing, or writing to learn, does not always have to take up your class time.  It is also implemented in assignments that students complete outside the classroom and, herein, lies its lasting value.  For example, you could give your students specific guidelines for reading which ask them to respond in specific ways in their journals.  Such responses may include asking them to raise questions about the reading, either questions about understanding or questions that raise issues.  Also, the students can be asked to respond in informal ways to questions that follow the readings in their texts.

Whatever the case, they will be responding in preparation for the next class.
Additionally, the journal is a good place to practice exam questions and answers. The journal can be used as a place to summarize and respond to articles for the course. It can also be used as a place where students define terminology from the course.

The most difficult issue with writing to learn is what to do with it, how to evaluate it. Because writing to learn places the emphasis on thinking and not on grammatical correctness, grading can be made easy. The following grading strategies have been tried and have worked: the number of pages a student has written over a certain period of time may be counted; a change in the quality of the student's insight can be observed; a simple credit/no credit grade can be used; the check, check-plus, check-minus system is also used; and last, points on a scale of 0 - 3 that convert to a grade at the end of the semester can also be used.

Writing to learn is for the students more than it is for the instructor. With this in mind, the activities are designed so that they will only take a minimal amount of time to grade. The journals will be looked over very quickly, generally providing students with an arena for learning and for experimenting with ideas that is a relatively "no-fail" situation.

WORKS CITED Chapter 2

Irmscher, William F. Teaching Expository Writing. New York: Holt, Rinehart and Winston, 1979.
Kinneavy, James L. A Theory of Discourse. New York: W. W. Norton and Company, 1971.
Larson, Richard L. "Teaching Before We Judge: Planning Assignments In Composition." Writing Teacher's Sourcebook. Eds. Gary Tate and Edward P. J. Corbett. New York: Oxford University Press, 1981.
Lindemann, Erika. A Rhetoric for Writing Teachers. 2nd ed. New York: Oxford University Press, 1987.
McCrimmon, James M. "A Cumulative Sequence in Composition." Rhetoric and Composition: A Sourcebook for Teachers. Ed. Richard L. Graves. Rochelle Park, New Jersey: Hayden Book Company, Inc, 1976. 225-238.
Moffett, James. Teaching the Universe of Discourse. Boston: Houghton Mifflin, 1968.

# CHAPTER 3:
# LOCATING IDEAS:
# A BEGINNING BIBLIOGRAPHY

This chapter, the last few pages of this section, will begin to direct you toward the abundance of available resources on the pedagogy of composition. Like all bibliographies, the bibliography itself will lead you to many more resources. In addition, each chapter has a bibliography which will be helpful if you are looking for information about a specific topic in writing instruction.

The indicated (• ) items are especially useful for the beginning teacher who is not sure quite where to begin.

Anson, Chris M., ed. Writing and Response: Theory, Practice, and Research. Urbana, Illinois: National Council of Teachers of English, 1989.

• Bizzell, Patricia, and Bruce Herzberg, eds. The Bedford Bibliography for Teachers of Writing. 1987 ed. Boston: Bedford Books, 1987.

Bizzell, Patricia, and Bruce Herzberg, eds. The Rhetorical Tradition: Readings from Classical Times to the Present. Boston: Bedford Books of St. Martin's Press, 1990.

• Bridges, Charles W., ed. Training the New Teacher of College Composition. Urbana, Illinois: National Council of Teachers of English, 1986.

• Cooper, Charles, R., and Lee Odell. Evaluating Writing: Describing, Measuring, Judging. Urbana, Illinois: National Council of Teachers of English, 1977.

Corbett, Edward P. J. Classical Rhetoric for the Modern Student. 3rd Ed. New York: Oxford University Press, 1990.

• Donovan, Timothy, R., and Ben W. McClelland, eds. Eight Approaches to Teaching Composition. Urbana, Illinois: National Council of Teachers of English, 1980.

• Duke, Charles R., ed. Writing Exercises from the Exercise Exchange. Vol. 2. Urbana, Illinois: National Council of Teachers of English, 1984.

Elbow, Peter. Embracing Contraries. New York: Oxford University Press, 1986.

---. Writing with Power. New York: Oxford University Press, 1981.

---. Writing Without Teachers. New York: Oxford University Press, 1973.

Emig, Janet. The Composing Processes of Twelfth Graders. NCTE Research Report No. 13 Urbana, Illinois: National Council of Teachers of English, 1971.

Fulwiler, Toby, ed. The Journal Book. Portsmouth, New Hampshire: Boynton/Cook, 1987.

• Glaser, Elsa R. for Maryland Instructional Television. Teaching Writing: A Process Approach. Dubuque, Iowa: Kendall/Hunt Publishing Company, 1983.

Graves, Richard A., ed. Rhetoric and Composition: A Sourcebook for Teachers. New Rochelle Park, New Jersey: Hayden Book Company, 1976.

Harris, Muriel. Teaching One-to-One: The Writing Conference. Urbana, Illinois: National Council of Teachers of English, 1986.

Hillocks, George, Jr. Research on Written Composition: New Directions for Teaching. Urbana, Illinois: ERIC Clearinghouse on Reading and Communication Skills, 1986.

• Irmscher, William F. Teaching Expository Writing. New York: Holt, Rinehart and Winston, 1979.

Kaplan, Rebekah, and Catharine Keech. Showing-Writing: A Training Program To Help Students Be Specific. Bay Area Writing Project Classroom Research Study No. 2. Berkeley: University of California, Bay Area Writing Project, 1980.

Kinneavy, James L.  A Theory of Discourse.  Englewood Cliffs, NJ:
    Prentice-Hall, 1971.

• Koch, Carl, and James M. Brazil.  Strategies for Teaching the
    Composing Process.  Urbana, Illinois: National Council of
    Teachers of English, 1978.

Lawson, Bruce, Susan Sterr Ryan, and W. Ross Winterowd, eds.
    Encountering Student Texts: Interpretive Issues in Reading
    Student Writing.  Urbana, Illinois: National Council of
    Teachers of English, 1990.

• Lindemann, Erika.  A Rhetoric for Writing Teachers.  2nd ed.  New
    York: Oxford University Press, 1987.

• Long, Littleton, ed.  Writing Exercises from Exercise Exchange.
    Urbana, Illinois: National Council of Teachers of English,
    1976.

Moffett, James.  Teaching the Universe of Discourse.  Boston: Houghton
    Mifflin, 1968.

• Myers, Miles, and James Gray, eds.  Theory and Practice in the
    Teaching of Composition: Processing, Distancing, and
    Modeling.  Urbana, Illinois: National Council of Teachers of
    English, 1983.

Rico, Gabriele Lusser.  Writing the Natural Way: Using Right-Brain
    Techniques to Release Your Expressive Powers.  Los Angeles:
    J. P. Tarcher, Inc, 1983.

Shaughnessy, Mina P.  Errors and Expectations: A Guide for the
    Teacher of Basic Writing.  New York: Oxford University Press,
    1977.

Spear, Karen.  Sharing Writing: Peer Response Groups in English
    Classes.  Portsmouth, New Hampshire: Boynton/Cook
    Publishers, 1988.

Tate, Gary, ed. Teaching Composition: Twelve Bibliographic Essays.
    Fort Worth, Texas: Texas Christian University Press, 1977.

---, and Edward P. J. Corbett, eds. The Writing Teacher's Sourcebook. 2nd ed. New York: Oxford University Press, 1988.

Winterowd, W. Ross, ed. Contemporary Rhetoric: A Conceptual Background with Readings. New York: Harcourt Brace Jovanovich, 1975.

In addition to these books, there are numerous excellent journals available. Some of these journals report primarily basic research, while others report applied types of articles. Basic research articles focus on theoretical issues and processes of composition and rhetoric while applied types of articles address pedagogical issues as they relate theory to practice. Check the periodical section in your library for these.

Last, if you join The National Council of Teachers of English, you will receive notice about new publications in the field and conferences you might consider attending that address issues of research in and teaching of composition.

# PART II TEACHING: THE EARLY DAYS

For someone who is new to teaching writing, the first few days of classes can pose some questions: What have I gotten myself into? What do I do? Where do I begin? How does all this get started? Rest assured that it all falls together quite quickly and systematically.

This section will help you get over these fears and through the first few days of classes. One very nice aspect teaching writing is that once your classes are rolling, they take on a life of their own because the process is repeated several times over the semester, so once your students have completed one full assignment, you can reflect on it, refine it, and repeat it with new material and a new assignment. This characteristic is exactly what makes the beginning days important because if you get off to a good beginning, you will most likely have a rewarding semester. (Even if you get off to a rough beginning, you will most likely have a rewarding semester--teaching writing is like that!)

Among the topics that this section covers are the following:

- setting your class's tone;
- taking care of administrative hoopla;
- checking the student roster;
- explaining your syllabus;
- pointing out important policies and procedures;
- encouraging talking and writing right off the bat;
- having students meet students;
- immersing students in writing and collaborating;
- collecting an assessment of student writing;
- teaching students how to elaborate and use detail; and
- teaching students to review work-in-progress.

I should also mention that the classes that are described in this section are one-hour-and-twenty-minute classes that meet twice a week. As I stated in Chapter 1, you may find yourself with another setup (e.g., fifty minute classes that meet three times a week).

# CHAPTER 4:
# THE FIRST DAY OF CLASS

## SETTING THE TONE

Your first class meeting should begin to set the tone for your entire course. While this sounds like an ambitious goal, it is one that you and your students can easily accomplish. Notice that it is you AND your students that give this class its tone: Teaching writing and doing writing are, neither one of them, solitary activities, but activities that we want our students to view as collaborative. As a result, you will want your students to take responsibility for the class's success as much as you do.

This collaborative approach to teaching and learning may be a new concept for most of your students: most will come to enjoy it and learn to rely on their classmates and friends for feedback as they write; one or two might think it offensive initially. On the other hand, some hold their frustrations inside: I once got a letter from a student after the semester was over saying that he had not signed up for a team sport! Had he mentioned this to me during the semester, I could have explained to him why writing is taught in a workshop environment that makes collaboration become a natural part of the writing process.

What relates all this to the first day of class is that it is essential to immerse your students immediately into the teaching methods that you'll use for the entire semester. Roger Garrison gave the following advice:

> In your first class meeting, after the inevitable housekeeping jobs of checking names against real bodies, and the rest, . . . put the group to work immediately . . . and without much comment, on what the course is all about: writing (9).

Garrison believed that students learn from the very onset that the course was about writing and little else. His method for showing students this was to get them writing, without talking to them about the value of learning to write or about classroom policies and procedures. Garrison was probably accurate in claiming that students won't believe your sermons about writing's value in their lives anyhow.

The remainder of this chapter discusses some options for your own class. Since feeling comfortable with your persona in the classroom is crucial to the class's success, you may want to adopt the Garrison first-day approach; on the other hand, you may want to choose other activities from among the following possibilities:

- distribute and discuss the syllabus;

- have students get to know one another; and

- get students writing.

It is possible to do a bit of all of these--which is my preference.

## ADMINISTRATIVE HOOPLA

Getting your class well organized is an important first step. This includes making certain that your students are in the right place, reviewing the syllabus, explaining your policies and procedures, and answering student questions.

## RIGHT PLACE, RIGHT TIME

Make certain that all of the students are in the proper class: have the students check your class title, section number, and room location against their registration information. Since at most colleges multiple sections of the same Freshman English course are offered at the same hour, students can easily get in the wrong place at the right time. If they are in the wrong class for too many class periods, their chances of success in the appropriate class diminish rapidly.

You'll hope to have a class roster of officially registered students on the first day, but often these rosters do not get to you before your first class meets. If this is the case, have students sign in, being sure to include their names and social security numbers. By the second class, you'll have been able to check your class roster against the real faces.

Don't lose patience or feel as if the registrar has something against you personally if the class constituents seem to change every day for two weeks or so. This variability is not unusual while students are settling their schedules. You, however, must press on with the business of your class despite these administrative inconveniences.

Once you have ascertained that you and your students are all in the right place at the right time, you might continue with the day's events by passing out and discussing the syllabus, which includes your statement of policies and procedures.

## THE SYLLABUS

Like most teachers, many writing teachers feel compelled to distribute the syllabus and review it carefully with their students. Since the syllabus that you distribute does serve as a legally binding document at most institutions, teachers like to point out the important features of the policies, procedures, and assignment calendar that are contained in the syllabus.

When you discuss the syllabus, be certain to cover specifically those policies that can get a student into trouble, i.e., cause him or her to be dropped from your course or fail your course. By pointing out that you want students to succeed in your course and that you want them to be sure to understand what can cause them trouble, you establish a collaborative and supportive atmosphere from the beginning.

## ATTENDANCE POLICY

Since much of the writing that students do they do with one another during class, attendance becomes a critical part of students' learning to write. Thus, many writing teachers maintain attendance policies because so much of teaching writing depends upon people being in class.

For example, imagine that rough drafts are due today. Your plan is to have students read one another's drafts, comment on them, and make recommendations for revising. You have carefully composed groups of students so that strengths and weaknesses are balanced, and your students are set up both to give and to receive useful feedback. Then, one-third of the class pulls "no shows." Not only will your time and effort preparing being wasted, but you will be irritated. Most importantly, the absent students will not benefit from having their classmates read, review, and respond to their work in progress.

With this in mind, set a policy for students' attendance in your class, and be certain that the students understand the policy, especially how they can get themselves into trouble in your course by missing classes. Explain to them what constitutes an absence, even though this may seem obvious to you. Also explain plainly and firmly what will happen to them and their grade if they are in violation of the policy.

Attendance policies include such issues as coming late, leaving early, coming unprepared (which can be considered an absence), and legal or religious holidays as excused absences. A word of warning if you intend to have an attendance policy: the easiest method is NOT to differentiate between excused and unexcused absences. This attendance policy protects you from acting as a judge over what can be considered acceptable or not as an excuse for absence. Give the students what seems like a reasonable number of absences; Many instructors offer students a week's worth of absences; Some departments have established policies that all instructors must follow. Call these "absences" and tell the students to use them cautiously because there is no such thing as an excused absence. When they have acquired one more than the allowable number of absences, drop from them from your course. Again, often departments have policies about how to handle students who have violated the attendance policy.

## LATE WORK

With writing being such an accumulative skill, students benefit most if they complete their work on schedule. Within writing projects and among individual writing projects, the sequence of activities and assignments is established to assist the student in his or her writing.

Thus, a student's being allowed to leave the simplest essay until late in the semester defeats the purpose of your placing it first, as does completing the free writing exercises after the essay just so he Haas something to turn in.

Whatever your policy will be regarding late work (e. g., "Late work is not accepted"), explain it clearly on the first day. No doubt, someone will put you to the test early in the semester. Once you have exercised your "LATE-WORK POLICY" by refusing to take someone's assignment, word will travel quickly, and you'll have little trouble with late work for the rest of the semester.

## PASSING THE COURSE

Explain what students must complete to pass the course if passing depends upon the completion of a certain set of work. For example, if you don't accept late papers, can a student get by without actually doing one of your major assignments? Does she have to complete it even though she'll get an "F" because it was late?

If you include informal writing assignments in your course

(such as a journal, textbook homework, in-class work, etc.), do students need to keep it and show it to pass the course? If you give them tests or quizzes, do they need to pass these to pass the course? If the English Department requires a final written exam, do students have to pass that exit exam to pass the course?

## SUPPLIES

Most of us require our students to buy an assortment of supplies. Reviewing these with students helps them tremendously. If you want students to have a pocket folder, show them what one looks like, or else many will still come with a regular manila file folder.

## CALENDAR

A large portion of your syllabus is the calendar of writing events for the semester. This should require little explanation, but a reference to major due dates and to multiple copy requests is often in order. Also, explain to students how you will figure their grade at the end of the semester: How will that 100% be divided up in the end?

## QUESTIONS

Needless to say, while you've been talking, the students have been reading the syllabus. Allow a few minutes for questions, and give complete answers. Remind students to read the syllabus completely; remind them that it will affect their lives; ask fro questions every day for a few days to make certain that your policies are clearly understood.

## TALKING AND WRITING: FIRST DAY ACTIVITIES

Having devoted some small part of your first class period (about fifteen minutes) to administrative affairs, you can now go on to a class activity. Both of the following activities work very well, get the class working as a group, and demonstrate the fact that time is valuable--even on the first day. Having students meet by interviewing and introducing one another is a dependable classroom ice-breaking activity, and also demonstrates that the students will need to rely on each other to succeed in class.  A writing activity that concludes with this collaborative effort also breaks the ice.


STUDENTS MEETING STUDENTS

In a class such as Freshman English, where knowing one another and feeling comfortable with one another is important to the class's day-to-day smooth running, interviewing and introducing classmates is more than an ice-breaker and time-user.  This activity gives students a feel for one another and the collaborative process immediately.  It can be done in any number of ways.  You can devote a large portion of one class period to completing the entire activity, or you can spread it over several days.

In either case, the procedure is simple and easy to tailor to your own preferences.

1.  Overview the activity--its procedure and purpose: Tell your students that they are going to need to learn one anther's names quickly, so the first thing you are going to do as a class is to conduct interviews.  Following their interviews, each student will introduce his or her classmate to the rest of the class.

2.  Ask students to pair up with their neighbors for this activity.  If there are an uneven number of students, you can either be part of the activity yourself or have one group of 3 students.

3.  Give the students several questions to ask a partner.  Questions such as the following are suitable and non-threatening on the first day of class: What is your name?  Your major, if you have one?  Do you have career aspirations?  Do you work; where?  What do you hope to learn from this class?  What is something unique about you to help others remember your name?

4.  Tell students to take notes on their conversations.

5.  Give them about 15 minutes to interview.  Tell them when 6-7 minutes has elapsed so that they can switch roles.

6. After the interviewing is complete, ask for volunteers to begin the introductions to the rest of the class. This can be done as formally or informally as you wish; that is, you could have pairs of students go to the front of the room, stand up, and speak, or you could simply have them stay seated and speak from their seats. On the first day of class, speaking from their seats is a good compromise.

7. You can vary this activity by also asking students to write up their introduction in a short letter to you and the class. If you do this, they can present their letter orally the next day. By doing this follow up, the time spent serves two purposes: getting acquainted and beginning to write.

### STUDENTS WRITING, STUDENTS COLLABORATING

While the whole class interviewing activity is a good way to get the entire class involved, the following writing activity gets students working independently and in small groups with their writing. Since working in small groups is probably something they'll do often in your class, this is also a good way to begin the semester--and it gets them writing. It is also a good place to have students practice free writing for the first time.

I use a handout called "The Values Questionnaire" which has been adapted from NCTE's book, Strategies for Teaching the Composing Process. The questionnaire comprises eight multiple choice questions, such as the following:

Of the following characteristics, which one do you most value in a friend?
  a. Honesty
  b. Loyalty
  c. A willingness to share  (Koch & Brazil, 30)

If you'd like to have students complete this activity, follow these basic steps (based on the advice of Peter Elbow in Writing With Power):

1.  Give students about five minutes to answer the eight questions. Students are told that there are, of course, no right or wrong answers.

2. Having completed the questionnaire, each student should select the one question about which he or she feels strongly.

3. Once each of the students has selected the question, have all of them flip over the questionnaire.

4. Introduce the idea of freewriting by giving these directions write for ten minutes without stopping, jotting down all the feelings, thoughts, facts, and/or ideas about the questions that you have.  Do this without stopping and without worrying about grammar, spelling, punctuation, etc.  JUST WRITE. (Remind students that the writing that they produce may not be what they think of as "good" writing, but that is not the goal of freewriting, rather quantity of writing is the goal.)

5. Tell them repeatedly to keep writing and not to stop: the goal is quantity.  In fact, some teachers give prizes to the student who produces the largest number of words.

6. While students are writing, you should do one of two things: if you feel as if you can manage more than one thing at a time, as you remind the students to keep writing,  walk among them encouraging those who are having difficulty.  It is also fine to just sit quietly at your desk, getting geared up for the next step.

7. At the end of the ten minutes, tell the students to stop writing: Finish the phrase or word that you have begun; then put your pens down.

8. The next phase of this activity asks the students to compose a short piece of writing.  Have students read their pieces of freewriting to themselves until they locate, what Peter Elbow calls the "center of gravity," a phrase or idea that seems to be repeating itself or looking for expression.  Then ask the students to compose a rough draft of a short piece of writing based on the concept they isolated from their piece of freewriting.  You might suggest that they think of a friend to whom they are writing a letter of which this will be a part. Don't allow them too much time for this either--15 or 20 minutes.

9. Last, and hopefully time will permit, have them convene in small groups, preferably organized around which of the questions they chose to answer. Ask each student to read his or her piece of writing to the group, and have the group select a favorite to be read to the class.

This activity doesn't necessarily lend itself to a piece of writing that is suitable for assessing students' strengths and weaknesses. It does, on the other hand, get the students immediately into looking inside themselves for ideas they have that are worth expressing. It also gets them sharing--reading, listening, comparing, and thinking--immediately. If your writing program requires that you obtain a piece of diagnostic writing on the first day, you might want to use this as your day two activity.

In a writing class, no matter what you do, the first day is a busy day, one that sets the pace and the tone for the remainder of the semester. The next chapter will outline some ideas for the next week of classes, after which the class pace will be established.

**WORKS CITED** Chapter 4

Elbow, Peter. Writing with Power. New York: Oxford University Press, 1981.

Garrison, Roger. How a Writer Works Instructor's Manual. New York: Harper and Row, 1981.

Koch, Carl, and James M. Brazil. Strategies for Teaching the Composition Process. Urbana, Illinois: National Council of Teachers of English, 1978.

# CHAPTER 5:
# THE NEXT THREE CLASSES

Having immersed your students (and yourself!) in what this writing class is all about in one exciting day, and with one or two more big days to go to complete the first week, you've gotten a good start. Congratulations!

This chapter will describe for you the other things you need to do at the very beginning of the semester to continue to get yourself off to a good and a well-informed beginning. The rest of this chapter describes three class days during which

- students complete a piece of writing (or other activity) that you will use to assess their strengths and weaknesses as writers and

- students are introduced to routine classroom activities.

## DAY 2: ASSESSING STUDENTS' WRITING ABILITIES

The initial sample of writing for assessment purposes (often also called diagnostic writing) should be collected as early in the semester as possible. In fact, at some colleges, you will be expected to collect the piece of assessment writing on the first day of classes, which would change the order of events as laid out for you in this book. Some first-year English programs enforce this first-day collection of assessment writing to make certain as early as possible that students are in the proper class.

Some teachers collect assessment writing more than once during the semester--e.g., at mid-term and at the end of the semester. If you want to compare students' progress, more assessment is better than fewer because you can adjust your teaching according to the assessment results.

The purpose of assessment writing is to examine students' writing and get a feel for the range of strengths and weaknesses that exist in your particular class. Remember, however, that this type of writing has limited, though extremely useful, value since it gives you information about how writers perform under particular circumstances.

A well designed writing prompt (the directions you give to students when they are composing a piece of assessment writing) will elicit writing from which you can determine a wide variety of useful

information according to Elsa R. Graser in <u>Teaching Writing: A</u>
<u>Process Approach</u>.  This information includes

- determining what the strengths and weaknesses of each student's writing are,
- hypothesizing on the causes of the weaknesses, and

- beginning to formulate a plan of techniques and strategies that will replace the weaknesses with strengths.

When you evaluate your samples of assessment writing,
remember that everyone does indeed have strengths, and by praising
and commenting upon a student's strengths you create a foundation
upon which the student will build as a writer.  In contrast, if you point
out all of a student's errors and weaknesses in a piece of writing, the
student will feel defeated at once--as if there is nothing upon which to
build.  Graser says, "The goal for beginners is fluency, and a teacher
who emphasizes a writer's errors teaches that writer to avoid making
errors by not writing.  Students know they have writing problems, but
seeing a list of weaknesses discourages the better writer and takes all
desire to write from the weaker student" (21).

## WAYS TO ASSESS STUDENT WRITING ABILITIES

The five basic types of assessment writing are identified in
<u>Teaching Writing: A Process Approach</u>: writing samples, standardized
achievement tests, functional or minimal competency tests, published
tests, and attitudinal surveys.

### THE WRITING SAMPLE

A writing sample is, from my point of view, the most valuable
kind of assessment writing because it actually asks students to respond
to a task and to compose a piece of writing.  Graser suggests that
students be given one of two options: an open topic that emphasizes
writing to a real audience who is interested in the topic or a list of
topics that the students choose from.  In either case, writers are directed
to think less about the mechanics of the writing than about the content
and organization (28).

Lindemann cautions us to be certain to give students a full

prompt when we ask them to write even a short in-class piece of writing.  If we ask students to compare the differences between living in the country and living in a city during a single class period, we offer them a poorly defined, unwieldy task, one that does not specify an audience (other than the teacher) or an aim (which students will assume to be for a grade); it also is so broad that the students will not know where to begin.

Instead of a broad and poorly focused prompt, we need to give them a writing task that is focused enough to be answered (engaging in all stages of the writing process if the students so desire) in the available time.  Include the following in the directions for the task: an aim for the piece of discourse, the mode you expect it to take, the form (e.g., a letter, an essay, etc) and the audience for the discourse.  For example, the following prompt takes these four criteria into consideration:

> Imagine that, as a recent graduation of City High School, you have been asked to write a letter to the Reader Speaks column of your high school paper.  For the most part, your piece will be read by high school students, especially City High's seniors.  You've been asked to write about getting ready for college.  Compare what you thought you'd need to do to get ready for college events such as registration, buying books, arranging for money, etc. with what you have found out you needed to do.  Include examples of what you did that you're glad about and what you wish you'd done.

## OBJECTIVE TESTS

A variety of kinds of objective tests can be used as assessment tools.  These include standardized achievement tests such as the California Achievement Test, competency tests such as ones that are published by individual states' educational agencies (e.g., the Texas Academic Skills Program Test), and Pre-and Post-Tests that sometimes accompany textbooks.

These kinds of objective tests, however, measure very limited writing ability since they actually test only a student's ability to edit another person's work.  Exceptions to this limitation occur occasionally, when students are asked to manipulate the content and organization of a full text.  Even so, the value of this type of test is limited essentially to measuring a student's knowledge of the mechanics of the language--spelling, punctuation, word usage, grammar.

## SENTENCE COMBINING TESTS

Sentence combining came about as the result of the work of Kellogg W. Hunt (1965, 1977), who speculated that a student's writing maturity could be determined by the number of ideas he or she can combine into a single sentence. This work was put into practical use by Frank O'Hare, John Mellon, and William Strong, all of whom have developed extensive exercises to assist students in maturing as writers.

To calculate the quality of writing maturity in a person's writing, Hunt devised a unit of measurement called a T-unit or terminable unit. The fewer the number of T-units per one hundred words, the higher the writer's syntactic maturity. A single T-unit includes an independent clause plus all of its descriptors (embedded or attached). The T-unit is so named because a piece of terminating punctuation (e.g., a piece of punctuation that ends a sentence such as a period) can be inserted by the scorer whether the student included it or not. For example, if a student writes, "The house is white, and it has red trim," the scorer identifies this as two T-units because a period (as terminal punctuation) can be placed after the word "white." The more mature writers would write, "The white house with red trim . . ."

A sentence combining test asks the student to take a string of simple sentences and combine them into as few sentences as possible, preserving all the original main ideas. Hunt, and others since him, used the following set of sentences as a sentence-combining test:

Aluminum is a metal.
It is abundant.
It has many uses.
It comes from bauxite.
Bauxite is an ore.
Bauxite looks like clay (95).

A student writing at the fourth grade level would use coordination (i.e., words such as "and" or "but") to combine these sentences. For example, a typical fourth grade response, according to Hunt, would be the following: "Aluminum is a metal and it is abundant. It has many uses and it comes from bauxite. Bauxite is an ore and looks like clay."

As students mature as writers (eighth to twelfth graders), they begin to use subordination more as in the following example from an eighth grade writer: "Aluminum is an abundant metal, has many uses, and comes from bauxite. Bauxite is an ore that looks like clay."

Eventually, Hunt writes, the most mature writers, skilled adult writers, use verbals more often: "Aluminum, an abundant metal with many uses, comes from bauxite, a clay-like ore" (Hunt, 95). Notice how the skilled adult writer has many more words in the one T-unit than either the fourth or eighth grade writer.

You might be wondering about the purpose of this kind of evaluation. Like other forms of assessment, sentence combining gives you a particular kind of information from which you determine the type of activity that will help your students continue to mature as writers. Thus, a sentence combining test will tell you whether a student could use work in the area of syntax. If your student is only combining at the fourth grade level, then some work in this area would be of definite value. In addition, sentence combining is an excellent way to teach punctuation and style. Like "showing writing," once you have taught students sentence combining, a simple phrase in the margin of their work-in-progress, "combine some sentences here," says a lot to the student.

## ATTITUDINAL ASSESSMENT SURVEYS

Often a student's strengths and weaknesses in writing can be traced to his or her earlier writing experiences, both at home and in school. With this in mind, teachers have found it useful to give students the opportunity to report on those experiences that have shaped both their attitudes towards writing and themselves as writers. One such survey (Graser, 31-32) asks the students to respond to several questions regarding their recent writing:

• In the last two years, how much did you write:

    In English class?

    In your other subjects?

    Outside of school for your own pleasure?

• What kinds of writing did you do in school?

- What kinds of writing did you do at home?

- How did you get ready to write?

- How did you go about revising what you wrote?

- How do you feel now about writing?

Other attitudinal scales, such as the Daly-Miller (1975), have the students agree or disagree with attitudes about writing with a check mark on a scale of 1 - 5, while still others have students respond with a true or false answer to questions about writing ("There is one best way to write."). This attitudinal information doesn't give the teacher much in the way of actual student composing, but these surveys do give the teacher helpful information about students' experiences and attitudes that can be helpful in assessing how to approach an individual student problem.

If, for example, a student believes that, "There is one best way to write," and he doesn't know what that "one best way" is or can't do it, you have valuable information. In conference, you can talk the student through this, explaining how writing is an individual skill, much of which can be learned, including how to approach and dissect a task to make it manageable. You can help that student feel that success in writing is possible for him. Answers to these survey questions also make good prompts for journal writing. You might ask the same student to use that statement, "There is one best way to write," as a first sentence in a journal entry, following that up with your comments to him about writing.


## A SAMPLE ASSESSMENT TASK

The example that follows asks students to compose a letter to the instructor about themselves, focusing on themselves as writers; the piece is then used for assessment purposes. This task synthesizes some of the kinds of assessment outlined above: a writing sample, attitudinal information, and writing skill. For example, the main thrust of the letter that students are asked to compose is about their writing experiences. This gives them an opportunity to point out their successes with writing as well as to vent any unpleasant experiences and attitudes they have toward writing. The task also asks them to think about writing and how they go about it. Thus, this task gives them a purpose and an interested audience, prescribes the mode and the form for the piece of writing, and clearly indicates what the audience is looking for.

---

### Assessment Assignment

Dear Student,

Welcome to Expository English Composition--English 3111!

I'd like you to introduce yourself to me in a letter. When you do this, include interesting and useful information about yourself, especially about yourself as a writer.

After you have introduced yourself to me briefly, since this is a writing course, I'd like you to begin thinking about your own writing as it is at this very moment. What kinds of things get you writing, both in school and out of school? Can you recount a writing experience that shaped how you feel about writing? Do you have writing that you are proud of?

Now, recall the last piece of writing that you composed--an assignment, a personal or business project, but not personal letters or diary entries. What was this piece of writing and did it have a name or title? Consider the reason you wrote it, when you wrote it, how you went about writing it.

How did you go about writing this last piece of writing? Did you use any pre-writing techniques (brainstorming, listing, clustering, or others); did you use notes, outlining, drafting, etc? Is this method your usual approach to a writing task?

* Did you think about the reader when you wrote?
* Can you make any other observations about your writing?
* Is there anything else that you'd especially like for me to know--about you or your writing?

Though this piece of writing will not be graded, it will give me an idea for how you write, what your strengths and weaknesses as a writer are, and what you think of writing in general. So, write your best in a letter to me. I look forward to hearing about you.

Sincerely,


Your Instructor

At the most, assessment writing will probably take about forty-five minutes of your class time. If you have an hour-and-twenty-minute class, you'll have time remaining. This is a good time to begin discussing the text or to practice a pre-writing activity. Clustering is fun and even after a taxing writing assessment, students manage to cluster with no problem.

## RESPONDING TO THE ASSESSMENT

Respond to your students' assessment writing immediately--by the next class. This helps you and the student in a number of ways: if the student does happen to be in the wrong level of composition, you can quickly place him or her in the correct class; you learn immediately the level at which your students are writing, and you can begin to revise your teaching plans, if need be, accordingly. Also, students immediately know what their standing in the class is--an important issue especially for first-semester college students who often are afraid of college work--and students too can plan what they need to do to succeed in your class.

When it comes to giving your students feedback about this initial assessment of their writing ability, you have several options for HOW you respond to it. See the chapter on evaluation in this book for more information about each of these methods of responding to your assessment of students' writing abilities:

- If the assessment was a writing sample, return the piece of writing with a holistic evaluation;

- For any of the methods of assessment, you can call students in for individual conferences, taking a few minutes (about 5-10) to discuss the strengths and weaknesses that you see in their writing;

- You can give them no formal response. In this case, don't return the assessment; keep it in a folder labeled with the student's name. In the folder include notes that you make on a separate piece of paper that the student does not necessarily see. Use these notes to decide what the student will work on over the course of the semester; record the student's progress on future papers. Make notes about the problems that have been overcome, the new work you want the student to do.

Since a student can't overcome all of his/her writing problems in one essay, this method keeps you in touch with where you wanted the student to concentrate (Lindemann, 207).

• Use a combination of the above: keep a record in individual folders; call the student in for conference, and/or provide the student with an evaluation that begins to guide him or her in writing projects. For example, see the form suggested in Chapter 2.


DAY 3: TEACHING ELABORATION AND DETAIL

In addition to regular textbook readings that you'll want to integrate into your daily activities, the next two days can be used to introduce students to some additional important and routine activities.

Since both creating detail and evaluating one another's drafts are central to a course such as this, I spend a concentrated period of time at the beginning of the semester introducing students to these activities and practicing them before I give them their first major writing assignment.


DISCOVERING DETAILS

One of the most important skills that you can provide for your students is practice in creating and using details, elaborating on their claims by being specific. They often don't know where to locate details, how much or how little to include, and so on. They think that if they tell you, "The party was great!!!" you immediately have a shared perception of the party that is equal to theirs. While there are a number of ways to teach students how to use detail to be specific and to elaborate a generalization, the most immediately useful technique I have found is "Showing Writing" (See Caplan; Caplan and Keech) where the point is made: "show me, don't tell me." Show me what a great party is like; help me to experience it from your shoes.

I introduce students to "showing writing" as soon as the administrative hoopla and the assessment writing are out of the way. I also persistently use it throughout most of the semester because one of the things that makes it so valuable is its universal application--the words "show me" in the margin of even a doctoral dissertation make their point quickly and clearly.

The success of using a technique such as "showing writing" depends on using it regularly. For instance, Caplan recommends that students be given daily practice expanding a generality, which she calls a "telling sentence." So, I give them a single telling sentence for homework each day for a period of time; they must develop this telling sentence into a paragraph. I also tell them to avoid using the telling sentence or the words from the sentence in their own paragraphs. For example, if I give them the sentence, "The cafeteria was messy," I ask them not to use either the sentence or the word "messy." I might even encourage some of them to avoid using the word "cafeteria."

In Showing-Writing: A Training Program to Help Students Be Specific, Caplan and Keech provide a menu of telling sentences to use as practice with students. These sentences are familiar to students, and this familiarity makes them effective in eliciting students' showing paragraphs. Some of Caplan's (1983) sentences are the following:

- She has a good personality;

- The concert was fantastic;

- The party was fun;

- I was embarrassed;

- My parents seem angry;

- My room was a mess (Caplan, "Showing" 230).

As Caplan points out, each of these sentences has the qualities of a thesis sentence for an essay, that the student must elaborate upon to support.

I have students keep their showing writing exercises as part of their English notebook, but unlike some journal or notebook writing, showing writing is written to be shared. I begin each class period by collecting students' showing writing pieces. I then read, at random, five of them aloud to the class, and as a class we evaluate the use of detail in each of these five. We respond exclusively to the content of the piece, asking ourselves the following questions, as Caplan recommends: Where has the author had success using details? Where were the details needed? As the days go by, the random selection for reading these paragraphs becomes a bit less random since I try to read students' work aloud that has not yet been read.

Again, using Caplan's recommendations, I grade the papers that I have read with an A, B, or C, and quickly add a comment that was made by the class. Caplan recommends taking about ten seconds to do this. Those that were not read get a "check" in the gradebook, those not done get a "0."

Each set of showing sentences is keyed to the type of essay the students are preparing. For example, when we write an evaluative essay, the showing sentences are like these: MacDonuts are the best donuts in town; my computer is the best model to buy; Roger Rabbit is the neatest movie I ever saw.

To introduce showing writing, I do two things: (1) I give students two paragraphs--one with lots of details and one without, preferably about the same topic. Caplan has some good examples that you can read aloud or put on an overhead transparency. (2) I use the "FRISKY SHAGGY DOG" exercise that I have outlined in the sample lesson plan in Chapter 1 of this book.

This work with showing writing leads directly into the next event: students practice reading and commenting on their classmates' work-in-progress.

## DAY 4: TEACHING STUDENTS TO READ STUDENTS' WRITING

Teaching students how to read other students' work-in-progress is one way to demonstrate how important feedback is as a piece of writing unfolds and how much useful advice a reader can give a writer. Since you'll have an initial rough draft coming in before too long, have students practice reading and commenting on one another's work early in the semester.

As students begin to draft their essays, you might ask them for permission to have copies of their work-in-progress so that you can use them as examples in another semester. This helps build your stockpile of examples that are specific to your own assignments, and it usually flatters students as well, but DO get their permission by having them complete and sign a written request. For informal use of students' work, I write a note on the student's paper, asking for a copy of the paper and permission to use it as an example during another semester. I keep a copy for my records, and assume if they provide me with the copy, I have permission. For more formal use of students' work, such as for national publication in a book such as this or in an article discussing student work, a written permission slip protects you and the student's rights. Some instructors make a consent form a part of their syllabus, giving them a carte-blanche approval to use any writing produced by students during the semester.

To begin teaching students how to read and respond to their peers' work-in-progress, I distribute copies of the draft that follows:

> A good lesson that I learned was that drinking beer or alcohol could lead me into problems that I had never dreamed of. It took me from my first day in high school til before entering to college to decide what the problem was. It was my excessive drinking of beer. I wouldn't drink it to have a good time but to get drunk.
>
> I first started to drink beer when I became a sophomore in high school. It was what everyone was doing and so I decided to try it. It was fun at first getting together with jock friends on weekends to go buy a six pack each. I would have a beer or two and I would already be drunk as time went on, I would have to increase the intake just to get a buzz.
>
> Before entering high school I was an "A" and "B" student. I would always do my homework on time and study for tests. Partying with friends in high school changed all that. I was still able to keep up with my A's and B's as a sophomore but when I became a junior and senior my grades changed to C's-D's and even F's. I didn't care anymore for studying and doing homework. I even changed friends.

In addition, I distribute copies of peer review worksheets like the ones the students will use to review one another's work. For the expressive essay, of which this is an example, I give them the following questions, dividing questions one through five between two editors for each person's work, and having each editor answer questions six, seven, and eight:

> 1. Does the author make the significance of this event clear? If yes, summarize that significance. If no, suggest how the writer can better communicate this event.
>
> 2. Comment on the organization of this paper. If you think it is well organized, tell what you liked about it. If you think it needs to be better or differently organized, tell the writer about this.

3. After reading this essay, is there anything more that you would like to know? Tell the writer what he or she should add before the final draft.

4. The beginning of a paper has to interest the reader immediately if it is going to succeed. Read the first sentence of the paper and rate its "appeal factor" on a scale of 1 to 10. Give the writer advice on how to make it a 10.

5. Comment on the conclusion to the essay. If it is effective, state what you like about it. If it could be more effective, show the author how it can be improved.

6. What one recommendation would you make to the writer about this paper?

7. What did you like best about this essay? Why?

8. On the draft underline the "telling" sentences that could be improved by "showing."

Having distributed copies of the essay and the review sheets, I place students into groups of three (four if anyone is left over). One member of the group is selected to read the essay to the group. Then, following both their own intuition and the guide that I have prepared for reviewing their peers' work-in-progress, the small groups of students analyze the sample student draft that I have given them. Since, unlike the days when the students will read one another's drafts, we are all now reading the same essay, I assign one of each of the first five questions to a particular group to work on in detail rather than having all groups do all questions. After about twenty minutes, the class reconvenes, and each group reports their recommendations to the class. As a class, we discuss the changes that each group has recommended.

Additionally, when they identify "telling sentences" in the draft, I ask the small groups each to compose a "showing paragraph" from the sentence they have identified. This is especially useful for them when they are working on their own drafts.

Last, I give them copies of the revised draft, a portion of which follows:

I stood next to a parked car with my hands on the hood and my feet spread apart, wondering what was going to happen to my friend Bobby and I.  A bright street light shone above our heads only to humiliate us among some passing friends who stared awhile.  A friend, Gus, asked, "Can we do anything to help?"  I turned my head sideways and replied in a shivering voice, "No, it's all right."  My throat was cramped up so tight that I didn't speak correctly, but Gus understood what I had said.

We discuss how peer review helped the student writer of the sample essay and what a different final product he composed, having gotten useful and honest feedback from his readers.  Next time they will be that much closer to doing this with their own drafts.  I remind them that even a great paper can be improved in some way, for writing is never truly completed.

## A LAST WORD . . .

The preceding information about teaching days one through four is information that you'll tailor to your own teaching style.  You might, for example, teach day two first, day four a week later; you might mix and match having parts of each of these sample days occur over a longer period of time.

Additionally, as you begin, you'll have textbook work to add to these concepts, as well as practice in freewriting and prewriting. (See the chapter on prewriting in this book for a variety of prewriting activities.)  In a writing class there is always PLENTY to do.

WORKS CITED Chapter 5

Caplan, Rebekah.  "Showing, Not Telling."  Theory and Practice in the Teaching of Composition: Processing, Distancing, and Modeling.  Eds. Miles Myers and James Gray.  Urbana, IL: NCTE, 1983. 226-238.

---, and Catharine Keech.  Showing-Writing: A Training Program to Help Students Be Specific.  Classroom Research Study no. 2. Berkeley: Bay Area Writing Project, University of California, 1980.

Daly, John A., and Michael D. Miller.  "The Empirical Development
    of an Instrument to Measure Writing Apprehension."
    Research in the Teaching of English 9 (Winter 1975): 242-56.
Graser, Elsa R.  Teaching Writing: A Process Approach.  Dubuque,
    Iowa: Kendall/Hunt Publishing Company, 1983
Hunt, Kellogg W.  "Early Blooming and Late Blooming Syntactic
    Structures."  *Evaluating Writing: Describing, Measuring,
    Judging.*  Eds. Charles R. Cooper and Lee Odell.  Urbana, IL:
    NCTE, 1977. 91-104.
---.  Grammatical Structures Written at Three Grade Levels.  Urbana,
    IL: NCTE, 1965.
Lindemann, Erika.  A Rhetoric for Writing Teachers.  2nd ed. New
    York: Oxford University Press, 1987.
Mellon, John C.  Transformational Sentence-Combining: A Method for
    Enhancing the Development of Syntactic Fluency in English
    Composition.  NCTE Research Report, no. 10.  Urbana, IL:
    NCTE, 1969.
O'Hare, Frank.  Sentence-Combining: Improving Student Writing
    without Formal Grammar Instruction.  Urbana, IL: NCTE,
    1973.
Strong, William.  Creative Approaches to Sentence-Combining.
    Urbana, IL: NCTE, 1986.

# PART III
# TEACHING: STUDENTS WRITING ESSAYS

Teaching students to write essays is another one of those tall orders: the fruits of your labors will be borne out in classes of all descriptions across campus for the students' next four years. Given these diverse disciplinary needs, the students whom you teach need to be exposed to a variety of writing techniques and strategies. Not the least of these techniques is exposure to the writing process itself, that is, the various ways of getting from the assigned task, through the blank page, and on to some finished prose.

Sometimes this is a lengthy process and the students will engage in many of the prewriting, drafting, and revising strategies that are described in this book and perhaps in your textbook as well. Other times, the student will be faced with an urgent need to write quickly or even on the spot. Your students need to be prepared to do both, to understand how to tackle each kind of writing problem and to make informed choices as they approach an assignment.

Generally speaking, students have composed quickly more often than they have composed over a period of time. They have written more exams and short essays than long writing projects, for example. Many, if not most, of your students will not have purposefully engaged in the writing process at all, which is why it is treated so completely in this book. Systematically engaging each step of the writing process is not the only way to approach writing successfully, nor is it always the best or the recommended way. Often, writers compose successfully without a single prewriting event or without a single revision. On the other hand, engaging in some stages of the writing process nearly always facilitates a thoughtful and polished piece of writing. However, keep two things in mind: (1) not all tasks require nor do all writers need to engage in every step of the writing process; and (2) when the writing process is used, it is a recursive one, not a linear process. This means the writer moves back and forth, in and out of the stages repeatedly until he or she feels finished with the draft, rather than proceeding in lockstep fashion from one phase to the next.

This section addresses in detail many of the options you have as a teacher of the writing process. Even though the writing process is not linear, this section of the book is organized in the recognized stages of the writing process: prewriting, drafting, revising, and evaluating.

The main topics that Section III, "Teaching Students to Write Essays," covers are the following:

- teaching students to analyze their audience and purpose before writing

- preparing students to write by engaging a variety of unstructured and structured prewriting activities

- having students practice organizing their details and drafting their essays

- improving essays through revision (peer review, conferencing, proofreading, etc.)

- evaluating your students' essays (holistic, primary traits, portfolio, etc.)

# CHAPTER 6
# PREWRITING:
# PREPARING STUDENTS TO WRITE

Have you ever thought about how you write--how you actually go about attacking a writing task? Where do your ideas come from? Do you mull things over for a while? Do you jot your ideas down at what seems like odd times? Do you add, subtract, revise, throw things away?

This chapter presents prewriting and invention techniques-- some of which you are no doubt familiar with. In this chapter, I have divided the discussion of these techniques into two major groups-- unstructured prewriting activities and structured prewriting activities. The unstructured activities include strategies for tapping a writer's tacit knowledge, for breaking through writer's block, and for writing without worrying about correctness. These unstructured techniques are designed to get ideas down on paper quickly; generally the quantity of ideas and words is more important than their quality. On the other hand, the structured prewriting includes activities that ask students systematically to explore their subjects from a variety of perspectives. These structured systems include classical invention techniques (status, topics) and those systems from contemporary rhetoric that are also topical systems (for example, Kenneth Burke's Pentad; Young, Becker, and Pike's Particle, Wave, and Field; and Richard Larson's Questions).

What I call prewriting here carries a variety of labels in composition and rhetoric textbooks: invention, discovery, heuristics, percolating, rehearsing. I choose to talk about this stage as "prewriting" because the term is more inclusive, referring to everything that comes before the actual drafting takes place, but not to be misinterpreted, as William Irmscher says, as "no writing" (78). Rather, prewriting is the preparation and exploration that writers engage in before they actually begin to draft. It is a time when "Despite the fact that much of the data that is gathered may be discarded, the act of collecting makes possible associations that may not have otherwise occurred to the writer" (Irmscher, 78).

The instructor's role in teaching prewriting activities is to make the student's job of writing easier in two ways: (1) by creating and using activities that loosen students up and help them overcome internal blocks toward writing; and (2) by giving students external structural paradigms as ways to help them generate and discover ideas (Irmscher, 79). Some of our leading composition scholars have made comments about the importance of teaching prewriting techniques to our students:

- Prewriting helps us examine what we know; we recall ideas, relate old and new information, assess what the reader expects of us, and generally explore the problem from many angles (Lindemann, 24).

- Pretty clearly the difficulty of teaching invention is at the heart of teaching a student how to write. You can't do much about his unity, coherence, and emphasis if he has nothing to say (English, 136).

- In this context, honest means a serious attempt to get at the heart of a problem, to look at the many sides of a question, to take into account conflicting data, to consider the relative merits of alternative hypotheses, to concede weaknesses, if any, as well as claiming strengths in one's conclusions, and to admit that what one is proving is 'probability' rather than 'absolute truth.' . . . There cannot be honest inquiry without serious consideration of techniques of invention (Harrington, 182, 183).

- What is needed for the teaching of invention today, therefore, is a plan that will help the student explore his experiences to discover when it is important to speak out, and that will help him speak out effectively on those occasions. We need a plan that draws attention first to the experience and then to the task of communicating effectively (Larson, "Discovery," 127).

- If some of the activities in this process of achieving [intellectual] equilibrium are conscious and learnable, we ought to teach them; so far as we can, we ought to show students what strategies they use when they think and what they can do to think well. In short, we ought to teach students to formulate and solve problems as creatively and effectively as possible (Odell, "Piaget," 37).

- Composition teachers should show students how to explore, sensitively yet systematically, facts, feelings, values, and ideas in order to determine what it is they wish to say in their writing (Odell, "Measuring," 107).

- The prewriting process is largely invisible; it takes place within the writer's head or on scraps of paper that are rarely published.

But we must understand that such a process takes place, that it is significant, and that it can be made clear to our students. Students who are not writing, or not writing well, may have a second chance if they are able to experience the writers' counsel to write before writing (Murray, 381).

Convinced that teaching a variety of prewriting techniques is crucial to teaching writing, you may have already realized that there are many options from which to choose. You might already be asking, "How do I teach prewriting? How do I know which of these options to use and when? How many should I use during the course of a single assignment?" Addressing these questions, the next section of this chapter focuses on how to use prewriting in the classroom.

## HOW TO USE PREWRITING TECHNIQUES IN THE CLASSROOM

The successful use of prewriting techniques need not be a mystery. Tommy Boley (1989) recommends that students engage in prewriting until they have a firm hold on the SOAP. By this, Boley means that students should have a clear idea of what their Subject, Occasion, Audience, and Purpose are--their SOAP. Broadly speaking, you have given some of the SOAP information to the students with your assignment. However, each student should refine an assignment's audience and purpose to make it her own, establishing a specific and meaningful context from which to write.

The following example, provided by one of my students, demonstrates a student's use of the SOAP method. Having been given the first assignment of the semester to write an expressive essay, such as the one that is used in Chapter 1 of this book, the student has been asked to write about an incident, a phase, or a significant person in her life. She completes the following SOAP to guide her through the prewriting of her essay:

Subject:    My subject is going to be my third grade teacher, Mr. Holmes.

Occasion:    The occasion is the college newspaper's essay contest for freshmen.

Audience:        My audience will generally be students, faculty, and
                 staff at the college.  My audience will also be the
                 judges of the essays submitted by other Freshmen.

Purpose:         My purpose is to write an expressive essay that will
                 show my readers how much having Mr. Holmes for a
                 third grade teacher has influenced the way I look at
                 life, especially my own life and my self-esteem.  My
                 ultimate purpose is to write an essay that is good
                 enough to win the contest.

To use prewriting successfully in the classroom, you should use a variety of the techniques that are presented in this chapter. Using prewriting activities in an arrangement that moves from the less to the more structured helps students to generate a lot of data, some of which gets used, some of which gets discarded, some of which gets elaborated upon.  The key is for the students to generate a lot of information so that they have choices to make and so that they have more information at their finger tips than they ultimately need to write their papers.  It is important first to use an unstructured technique that will get the student thinking about either a prescribed subject or about what she wants to write about. The unstructured prewriting activities work well to assist students in the actual discovery of what information or what subjects are in their heads.

Once students have discovered a subject and some information related to it, the more structured prewriting activities work well. These activities help students to refine their theses, explore their topics from a variety of perspectives, and organize the material that they eventually gather.

The next sections of this chapter talk about students' exploration of audience and purpose, unstructured prewriting activities, and structured prewriting activities.

## TEACHING AUDIENCE AND PURPOSE IN WRITING

Audience and purpose are so closely linked that it is often difficult to know which a student should address first.  Addressing them in tandem often works well.  The essential question that students are answering is "To whom am I writing and why?"

Earlier in this book, I talked about specifying an audience and purpose for students' writing assignments.  Most likely, you will find the issue of audience and purpose discussed in the textbook that you are using, often describing the choices that students may make among a variety of audiences and purposes.  In fact, some texts provide very useful questions about audience and purpose (in the form of checklists) for your students to complete as part of the prewriting process.  You also might construct your own version--adding and subtracting questions that are specific to your current assignment--as handouts for students to complete.  Since not only what they are writing about, but also to whom they are writing directs students' selection of details and organizational patterns, describing their audience and purpose is an important part of the writing process.

Your guidance is also important, as always, since the idea of audience analysis will most likely be a new concept to your students. My advice is to run through this exercise thoroughly, maybe with several types of audiences, both as a class and in small groups before individual students attempt doing their own.


## ANALYZING THE AUDIENCE

Analyzing their audience is one of the most important skills--right alongside purpose--that students practice.  Without careful attention to their audience's characteristics, writers often fail to adjust the message for either the needs or the attitudes of their readers.  Often students fail to think of the potential for a hostile audience, an uninformed audience, a disagreeable audience, a dangerous audience, or even a neutral audience, resulting in essays that fall short of accomplishing their goals.

"What about me, the students' teacher, as an audience?" you might be wondering.  Your students have written to their teachers for years.  What you want to do is to help them now develop beyond the teacher-as-judge mindset, bridging the academic audience and preparing them to communicate in the nonacademic world.

Plenty has been written about ways to have students analyze their audience; for the most part, everyone advocates having students consider various characteristics of an audience.  Linda Flower suggests that all characteristics fall into one of three categories: the audience's attitudes towards the author and the subject, their personal or professional needs, and their knowledge, both in general and about the particular subject being written about (130-132).  Several useful schema have emerged, some of which follow.

Oftentimes, as teachers (and some textbooks do this too) we have students consider whether the audience for whom they are writing is a general one or a specialized one. Then, like Flower suggests, we ask students to jot down on paper the audience's background and knowledge regarding the subject, as well as their interests, beliefs, values, and attitudes. Many textbook authors put these audience characteristics into concrete and useful questions for guiding the student through the process of analyzing the audience. By asking students to respond to these questions, we challenge them to think carefully and in depth about to whom they are writing. Useful questions include the following:

- What audience am I addressing? Is my audience an individual or a group of people? If a group, is my audience a general one whose knowledge of the subject varies? Or is it a limited audience that shares the same knowledge?

- How can I capture the attention and interest of audience?

- What interests and attitudes should I take into account?

In the early stages of targeting the audience, you might also have students consider some other questions about their audience, such as the following, which I have adapted from John Lannon's Technical Writing, 4th ed.:

- About the audience's attitudes . . .

    What attitudes is the audience likely to hold towards me? Towards my subject?

    How old is the audience? What are their professions? How much education do they have? Is this a specialized audience? A general one?

    How will the audience react to my essay? Could they be hostile, offended, pleased, annoyed, appreciative, etc.?

- About the audience's needs . . .

    What is my relationship to my audience? How will the audience use what I write?

How much are they likely to know already about my subject?

What questions might my audience have about my subject? Have I answered them in my essay?

- About the audience's expectations . . .

  Does the audience expect the essay?

  How long do they expect it to be? What kinds of details would be appropriate for this audience?

  What kind of tone would they expect? How might they expect it to be organized?

  How do I hope to affect my audience? (34)

Last of all, having completed an assignment that incorporates some or all of the preceding suggestions, have students compose a paragraph or two describing their audience.

In "Topoi and the Problem of Invention," Wallace presents an outline of topics to have students consider when examining an audience. You might turn some of his recommendations into questions for students to consider when thinking about an audience. Wallace recommends that students consider the following:

- General condition

- Values
        the desirable
        the obligatory
        the commendable

- Value hierarchies
        group and institutional
        age
        individual

- Economic

- Educational

- Affective states: emotions, motives, feelings

- Political preferences

- The probable and possible
    assumptions and presumptions
    patterns of thought (121).

You may be wondering how to use this material with your students. Probably the most efficient thing for you to do is to create a worksheet for students to complete as they describe their audience. If you do this, you can tailor the worksheet to your own assignments. In lieu of worksheets, journal entries and class discussions can also be useful for analyzing audience, as can the aforementioned written paragraph.


DETERMINING THE PURPOSE

Having created a detailed portrait of the "To whom am I writing," students also need to contemplate "the why." The "why" is answered in part by your assignment, but beyond that, it is addressed more fully by the student who, in interpreting your assignment, finds his or her idiosyncratic, individual purposes for writing. According to many contemporary rhetorical and composition theorists, most writing (with the exception of literature) has one of three purposes: expressive, informative, or persuasive.

Having received an assignment that asks him to write for the school newspaper's competition about a personal experience, the student chould place this task into the "expressive" purpose; beyond this, however, he should place this task into a specific framework, more detailed than just "expressive." To do this, he might answer some of the questions that follow:

- What is my purpose in writing? Do I wish to express my feelings and beliefs? Am I writing to declare my position on an issue or to protest a practice, policy, attitude, or idea?

- Is my purpose to explore an aspect of the world, perhaps through an experience or observation of my own? Do I want to explore a problem by analyzing it and considering solutions to the problem? Do I want to propose my own solution?

- Do I want to give information about a person, place, or object? What use do I want the reader to make of this information?

- Do I want to achieve more than one purpose in writing? Do I want to give information about a situation? Do I wish to express my feelings and beliefs about this situation and, in addition, persuade my readers to accept and act upon them?

In conclusion, issues of audience and purpose are important ones in a writing class. Flower, in <u>Problem-Solving Strategies for Writing</u>, recommends that writers build bridges of shared expectations and common features with our readers. If your students know what attitudes and beliefs an audience holds, and his purpose is to persuade that audience, he will be more convincingly persuasive. Flower says, "The more these [knowledge, attitudes, needs] differ from your own, the more you will have to do to make him or her see what you mean" (131).

## TEACHING UNSTRUCTURED PREWRITING: FINDING A SUBJECT, EXAMINING ITS ANGLES

Unstructured prewriting activities, such as journal keeping, freewriting, brainstorming, clustering, and talking, all provide opportunities for students to explore their thoughts with few "how-to" rules. These are excellent ways for students to get started, to break through the blank page, to prompt thinking, to jar the memory, and to discover ideas and subjects that are lurking beneath the surface.

## JOURNALS

"Human beings find meaning in the world by exploring it through language" (Fulwiler, 1). As a result of this widely held belief, many writing instructors are using informal, speculative kinds of writing in their classrooms. To facilitate this kind of writing, instructors' use of journals has grown in popularity as teaching tools in many classes, especially writing classes.

## WHAT ARE JOURNALS?

Also called notebooks, logs, reading logs, writing logs, daybooks, commonplace books, or diaries, the journal can be a "catch-all" kind of place where students record a variety of writing activities: "true" journal responses, answers to exercises from their textbook or from your class exercises, prewriting work, drafting ideas, and so on. Journal writing was discussed in more detail in Chapter 1 of this book, where kinds of journal entries and ways to evaluate the journal were discussed.

In a writing class, the journal has many uses. You can have students write daily for ten minutes at the beginning of class. Assignments from the text can be included as journal entries. They can also be used as a notebook or workbook for the course where you ask students to keep their essay planning work--freewriting, outlining, exercises, and standard journal questions.

Since a journal can be puzzling to grade for a new teacher, knowing what Toby Fulwiler, in The Journal Book, describes as the characteristics of good journals is helpful. These qualities include features of the language that the student uses, kinds of mental or cognitive activities that the student engages in, and a variety of formal features. The following list summarizes these features as Fulwiler presents them:

- Language Features: The writer uses
        colloquial diction
        first-person pronouns
        informal punctuation
        rhythms of everyday speech
        experimentation (e.g., writer trying a new voice)

- Cognitive/mental activities: The writer
        makes observations
        poses questions
        speculates
        shows self-awareness
        igresses
        synthesizes ideas, courses, topics, etc.
        revises former thoughts
        listens, responds to, and understands class notes

- Formal features: The writer makes
  frequent entries
  long entries
  a chronology system of entries (2-3).

Fulwiler (5-6) reproduces The National Council of Teachers of English's "Guidelines for Assigning Journals." These include the following:

- Explain that journals combine features of both class notebooks and diaries. They are written in the first person, but are concerned with the course and its content.

- Ask students to buy looseleaf notebooks that can be divided into sections.

- Suggest that the students divide their notebooks into sections. The sections can be several parts of your course or they can be your course, other courses, private entries.

- Ask students to do short journal writings in class, and write with them.

- Use the writing that students compose in class to give credibility to what might be an ungraded assignment.

- Count but do not grade student journals--a number of points, a plus added to an essay grade, a resource for in-class exams.

- Do not respond to each entry. Skim them and respond to entries that concern you.

- At the end of the term have students number the pages, title each entry, compose a table of contents, and write an evaluative conclusion. This way, students review what they have written and reflect upon it.

## HOW DO YOU USE JOURNALS IN YOUR CLASS?

The following "Self-Discovery Journal" sequence gives the students a chance to "find out who they are and what they want to be in the future" (Bardas, 1).  In this sequence of thirteen entries, students are asked to write several entries in each of three categories: five entries called "Centerings" (focus on the present); four entries are "Reminiscences" (about the past); four entries called "Cinemas" (looking into the future).  The following are prompts for the "self-discovery" sequence discussed by Mary Louise Bardas in her article:

- Centering (Present, feelings): Brainstorm all of the emotions and sensations you have been experiencing lately.  Let them flow freely.

- Reminiscence (Past, place): Locate a place in your memory a place which has (and may still have) great meaning for you.  Brainstorm as much detail as you can.

- Reminiscence (Past, person): Find a person who had great meaning for you at some time during your past experiences.  Brainstorm all you can about this person.

- Reminiscence (Past, dialogue): Imagine a scene, as in a play, in which you talk about your current life situation with someone from your past.  After you have written the dialogue, reread it and summarize the meaning.

- Reminiscence (Past, myth or tall tale): Write a myth or tall tale about someone in your personal past: a family member, an ancestor, or someone else memorable.

- Centering (Present, thoughts): Brainstorm your world view: write freely about what the world seems to be like to you.

- Cinema (Future): Write a scene in which you star as a successful young college student or recent graduate who has clearly taken control of his or her life and circumstances, one who is enjoying the satisfaction of living through conscious choices.

- Cinema (Future): Write a milestone, an imagined obituary for yourself which sums up the major accomplishments of your ideal life.  It should reflect what you hope will be said about you when your life is concluded.

- Centering (Present, wants): Write down freely all the things you really want to do in and with your life. Be inclusive: let all your dreams and aspirations flow.

- Cinema (Future): Write for yourself an acceptance speech which you will deliver when you receive an award of great distinction: Nobel Prize, Pulitzer Prize, National Book Award, An Emmy, etc.

- Cinema (Future): Write a scene in which you star as a contented elder. Perhaps your grandchild or great-grandchild want to know what makes for a happy life.

- Centering (Present, reflections): Read back over everything you have written in your journal. Name the events, circumstances, and persons which have contributed most powerfully to your present outlook on life and your hopes for the future.

- Centering (Present, Assessment): Looking back through everything you have written, make a final list of your values, beliefs, attitudes, and goals at this moment. Are they same as your family's? Assess how realistic your feelings and ideas about the world are: What can you do this year to move toward your goals?

This series of journal entries moves students from thinking about their present lives to thinking about their pasts and their hopes for the future. In their final entries, they reread everything that they have written, think about it, and "assess how realistic their feelings and ideas about the world are, and to provide objective evidence that seems to corroborate or to negate their reality" (Bardas, 3). The "Self-discovery Journal" serves as a "heuristic and provides an idea bank for assigned writing, and it is a logical first step in a hierarchy of writing activities" (Bardas, 3).

The entries that you will read in students' journals will likely range from boring to sentimental and emotionally touching to what they hope will shock you. Your response to students' journal entries, however, should always be positive and encouraging. You might want to pose questions where you think a student can be pushed to think more about an issue. Often, instructors look upon these responses to journal entries as a dialogue between themselves and each student. They can build a kind of rapport that students get in few other classes, as well as let the student know that the journal really does matter.

A word of caution: Don't even try to read all the entries in every student's journal. You'll burn out, and miss opportunities to respond where you should or would want to. Generally, skim them, and stop when you see an important issue, idea, feeling, opinion to which you can respond.

## FREEWRITING

Freewriting is a prewriting technique that helps students tap into experiences and memories, sometimes very distant, for ideas about which they can write. Advocated by both Peter Elbow and Ken Macrorie, freewriting has subsequently been adopted by many teachers of writing as a valuable way to get students writing, especially to get them to get words on paper. Elbow states that, "Freewriting is the easiest way to get words on paper and the best all-around practice in writing that I know" (Power, 13).

### WHAT IS FREEWRITING?

In Writing Without Teachers, Peter Elbow describes the freewriting technique in this way:

> The most effective way I know to improve your writing is to do freewriting exercises regularly. At least three times a week. They are sometimes called 'automatic writing,' 'babbling,' or 'jabbering' exercises. The idea is simply to write for ten minutes (later on, perhaps fifteen or twenty). Don't stop for anything. Go quickly without rushing. Never stop to look back, to cross something out, to wonder how to spell something, to wonder what word or thought to use, or to think about what you are doing. If you can't think of a word or a spelling, just use a squiggle or else write, 'I can't think of it.' Just put down something. The easiest thing is just to put down whatever is in your mind. If you get stuck it's fine to write 'I can't think what to say, I can't think what to say' as many times as you want; or repeat the last word you wrote over and over again; or anything else. The only requirement is that you never stop (3).

Freewriting can be either focused or not.    Often focused freewriting comes after you or your student have selected a broad topic. In focused freewriting a student might freewrite about a particular subject (e.g., the teacher who has had a significant impact on your life), idea, or feeling.    In non-focused freewriting, the student just writes. Whatever the task, freewriting is never graded; if it is, it is no longer "free."    Thus, your students' freewriting should be free from criticism of any kind, editing, recommendations for revising, or grading. Freewriting entries can become a part of your students' journals, however.    In this way, you can be certain that the students are practicing this technique.    Also, you can and should have them freewrite frequently in the class.    This, if done for ten to fifteen minutes at the beginning of each class over a period of several weeks, makes writing a habit and also makes the point that writing class is a place where students write.

## FREEWRITING IN YOUR CLASSROOM

How do you use freewriting in your classroom?    The following suggestions might serve as either help or a springboard to your own freewriting exercises.

## AN OBJECT OR IDEA AS STIMULUS

For a freewriting exercise, Irmscher recommends bringing something to class that you can use to stimulate students' thinking. He suggests a picture, a piece of sculpture, or a short film.    To push students' minds, he recommends that you not only have them freewrite, but that you ask for something specific, such as "List 35 details" (82). Some people would call this brainstorming, not freewriting, but the point is the same: to get ideas down on paper in a quick and uncensored manner.

Freewriting can help your students find a subject about which to write.    By having them freewrite a couple of times and look for words or phrases that repeat themselves, students learn --through writing--to explore their subconscious for subjects to write about. Freewriting procedures will help your students to loosen up a bit, relieve them of what Irmscher calls, "mental uptightness" and find subjects of importance to them about which they want to write.

## A FINISHED PIECE OF WRITING

Elbow recommends doing two or three successive freewriting exercises to get a finished piece of writing quickly.  To do this, he says, students keep their possible topics in mind and do one or two freewriting exercises, trying not to wander from their topics. Sometimes digressions occur in the writing and they'll need to let them happen, for  digressions sometimes provide the writer with useful material.

After these freewriting exercises, students look at the writing and think about what they have written.  They, then, do another freewriting exercise focusing on the idea that most attracts their attention or the one that they wrote the most about.  Repeated three or more times, each exercise often results in better and better information about which to write.

Finally, students look at all of this freewriting for the rich and important words, phrases, and sentences.  They throw away the "garbage," and look carefully at what is left, adding what they need to in the way of transitions, organizational matter, stylistic editing, or content additions.  They'll most likely have a finished piece of writing.

As Elbow cautions, this is not foolproof, especially for new freewriters, but over the long term, more good writing than bad results.

## LOOP WRITING

This process is described in detail in Chapter 8 of Peter Elbow's Writing With Power.  Loop writing, says Elbow, "is a way to get the best of both worlds: both control and creativity . . . It is a way to focus that creativity on goals other than the ones you happen to carry around inside you.  Thus, it is especially useful if you can't think of much to write or are stuck with a topic that bores you" (Power, 59).  Elbow divides loop writing into two stages: "the voyage out" and "the voyage home."  In the voyage out, he provides thirteen ways to freewrite about a subject, gathering details and information for an essay.  These include the following:

- first thoughts--as fast as you can, put down all the thoughts and feelings you have about the topic;

- prejudices-- identify them in relation to your topic;

- instant version--disregarding the need for research or planning, write a first draft;

- dialogues--give your prejudices voices and have them converse;

- narrative thinking--good, if your thinking shifts, to write the story of your thinking: first, I thought this, then that;

- stories--include stories and events that you know or can imagine about your topic;

- scenes--focus on individual moments like a photograph;

- portraits--jot down descriptions of who comes to mind as you think of your topic?  These may bring good insights about your topic;

- vary the audience--write to someone besides the real audience for your paper;

- vary the writer--write as if you were someone with a different view on the topic;

- vary the time--write as though you were living in the past or the future;

- errors--write down things that you or others think but are false; "dangerous mistakes";

- lies--write down anything you can come up with, nonsensical stuff.

Generally, students won't need to use all of these choices for any one writing assignment, but practice with them gives them yet more perspectives from which to view a subject.

Once the voyage out is completed, the writer is ready to begin the voyage home.  The voyage home is essentially one of revising.  A student needs to read all that he or she has written.  While reading, Elbow recommends that the writer make notes in the margin, selecting the good bits and perhaps adding to these.  Reading through what the student has written might even reveal a thesis, the point the writer wants to make.

Then, the students need to think about the assignment, while examining their insights, and choosing the bits and pieces of information that are useful.  Last, they piece together a coherent essay.

### SEQUENCING AND SHARING FREEWRITING EXERCISES

Sequencing freewriting exercises in the classroom and having students share them with one another is another very useful way for students to discover what they have to say about a subject.  Donald Murray recommends that students respond to one another by focussing on questions about freewritten passages.  For example, he recommends that students freewrite for several minutes, then work in pairs to answer the question, "What appeared on the page that you didn't expect?"  After talking about this, students return to freewriting, which is followed by another question, "What idea do you want to develop in the next freewriting?"  This procedure continues, as students freewrite followed by answering questions in pairs or small groups.  Lindemann suggests the following questions: "What is the writing telling you?  How do you (the writer) feel about what is appearing on the page?  What do you (the reader) need to know that I haven't told you yet?" (79).

### LISTING, BRAINSTORMING, SORTING

Listing, brainstorming, and sorting are close cousins of one another, but each is specifically and independently a valuable discovery technique.  Each one provides the writer with an abundant supply of details.  Each begins as a somewhat focused exercise and ends with a supply of ideas about which the student might write.  As the teacher, you should demonstrate each of these prewriting techniques and the ways in which one of them can lead to another, for example, how listing can lead to brainstorming.

Let me illustrate how these are used by citing an example.  In the first unit of my course, one on expressive writing, I have students read the essay, "Miss Duling," by Eudora Welty.  In this essay, Welty is talking about one of her teachers and the significance of this teacher in her life.  Since one of the choices my students have is to write an essay focusing on a person, I have them do a series of discovery techniques to locate a possible subject for this essay.

First, I take about five to ten minutes and have the students LIST all of the teachers or other people who have been an important part of their lives.

Next, I have them SORT this list in some way. The key is to give them a forum for discussing ways to categorize these--as a whole-class discussion or as a small group activity--but not to tell them the categories that you (the teacher) see for sorting their information. If you give them too much direction, they might not be able to come up with their own categories. On the other hand, suggestions from other students are acceptable. This sharing helps them to learn to rely on one another as they write. This activity takes about ten to fifteen minutes.

Having sorted this list, students then select one person from their list and BRAINSTORM anything and everything that they can think of about that person. As is case with freewriting, they write quickly and plentifully, without concern for what they put down. The key again is to get lots of details, some of which they will discard, but many of which will be useful, eventually, in composing the essay. Often, the brainstorming is followed by sorting again. This process leads to the emergence of some pattern of details that the student has produced, indicating what he or she is most interested in writing about. Allow about fifteen minutes for brainstorming.

For example, Megan was preparing to write the first essay of the semester, an expressive essay. The class had read "Miss Duling" and were ready to prewrite for ideas for their essays.

First, in response to being asked to list all of the teachers that she could remember, Megan came up with the following list in five minutes, indicating really influential people:

| | |
|---|---|
| Mrs. Campbell | Mrs. Bingham |
| Mrs. Ayde | Mrs. Hulse |
| Mr. Kier | Mrs. Bush |
| Mrs. Widrig | Coach Vanderhoff |
| ◆Mr. Holmes | Manny |
| ◆Mrs. Mineau | Maureen |
| Mrs. Karl | Julie |
| Mrs. Kautz | Mrs. Villalobos |
| Miss Scoggins | Coach Alfaro |
| Nancy | Mrs. Brown |
| Mrs. Newsome | Mrs. Corrigan |
| Mrs. Bath | Matt |
| Mr. Wilhelm | Mrs. Barker |
| ◆Mr. Currey | Mrs. Schmidt |

Next, she found a variety of ways to sort the list: men and women; married and unmarried; pre-school, grade school, middle and high school; sports, math and science, humanities, music, other.

From this list of teachers, Megan chose to brainstorm about her third grade teacher, Mr. Holmes.     She produced the following assortment of brainstormed material:

Third grade, all-time favorite teacher.
Short, mustache, "in shape," light brown hair, casual dresser-- sport shirt and pants, blue eyes.
Nice, friendly, Celeron, jokes, stories, experiences. Explains assignments, sets the classroom mood/tone, students--his time and energy, extra tutoring after school.
Music, inspiring, caring, role model, kept my attention. Believed that everyone was special.  Built our self-esteem in a mega way.
A learning experience--made it easy to understand, interesting, taught us about life, amazing--encouraging--understanding, flexible teaching methods, admitted mistakes.
Blubber, fun, funny, peanuts were rewards, messy handwriting.
Memory--remembered me years later when I graduated and sent him a letter.
Around the world, spelling bees, eating worms, Fudge, arts and crafts, nurse's office.

In addition to brainstorming, sorting, and listing, this is a good place to insert another free writing exercise.  Since Megan so quickly produced a wide assortment of details about Mr. Holmes, she then free wrote about him to see what else she could uncover.  This is the result:

I was a 3rd grader--thought I knew it all . . . had the best teacher I've ever had.  Third grade was so many years ago for me.  I find some things about it hard to recall.  One thing stands clear--Mr. Holmes.  He was my teacher and my "pal." He taught me a lot of things--not just math, spelling, and History.   He taught us to like ourselves--glasses, braces, missing teeth, and all.  He read to us every day and always books about friendship, caring, self-respect, and self-esteem. Our confidence in our selves, our studies, and our activities was #1 w/ Mr. Holmes.  Strange things to try to be teaching 3rd graders--little 7 yr. old snots who fight & lie & cry & tease.

But, through the eyes of Blubber and Judy Blume we learned the "things" in life in a humorous way. I loved his class, his peanuts, his games, but mostly I loved him. He gave me a lot to use in later life--through high school and now in college. He pops into my mind.

These steps of listing, sorting, and brainstorming lead easily to another prewriting exercise, clustering (also referred to as mapping or tree diagrams).

CLUSTERING

What is a cluster?    A cluster is a visual and verbal representation of a student's potential piece of writing.    As a prewriting technique, the cluster has a number of advantages over the previously mentioned prewriting techniques because the student creates ideas, generates words and phrases, and organizes these into hierarchical relationships as he clusters.    For this reason, if students have time for only one prewriting activity as is the case in a timed essay, clustering is a winner.    If they have the luxury of engaging in more than one, clustering is an excellent followup to listing, brainstorming, and sorting.

One of the originators of clustering, Gabriel Rico, in Writing the Natural Way, describes the process in this way:

To create a cluster, you begin with a nucleus word, circled, on a fresh page.    Now you simply let go and begin to flow with any current of connections that come into your head.    Write these down rapidly, each in its own circle, radiating outward from the center in any direction they want to go.    Connect each new word or phrase with a line to the preceding circle.    When something new and different strikes you, begin again at the central nucleus and radiate outward until those associations are exhausted (35).

Rico claims that having her students prewrite by clustering has produced coherent, unified pieces that also demonstrate a sensitivity to patterns and rhythms of the language.    Also, she claims, her students seemed to punctuate and phrase more clearly and spell better (11).

While I have found all this to be true, I have also found that by using clustering, I can demonstrate visually what clear organization looks like, facilitating well-organized final essays. For students who have difficulty understanding how to write a unified paragraph, clustering provides a visual representation of the paragraph before the student writes it.   The example of clustering that follows, Megan's prewriting for an essay describing how a particular teacher (the third grade teacher, Mr. Holmes) has had an impact on her life, demonstrates what I mean.   Megan begins with the nucleus or the main idea in the center bubble.   Then from that, she branches the main reasons for this teacher having such an impact on her life (from her brainstorm and sort session).   She concludes by using examples to show how each of these reasons is true.   Once she has created this cluster map, she can look at the main branches to create her thesis sentence and begin to build paragraphs, each one developing one of her main ideas about this teacher.

Since clustering can visually display the hierarchy of ideas, it is also an excellent way to show students where they need more details and examples on a more specific level of the paragraph.   Because

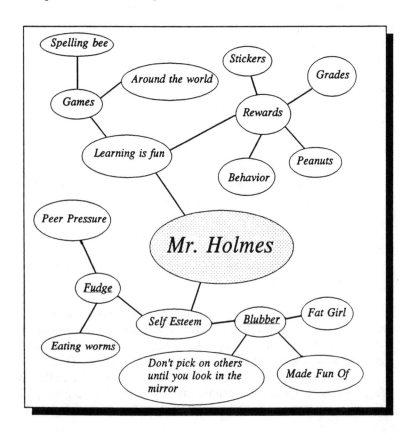

subordination of ideas (primary, secondary, tertiary) is apparent through the cluster bubbles and branches, students quickly see where they need more material, where they have too much, where an idea can be combined with another, or where an idea needs to be discarded. I tell students that, if they have a good cluster map, they can fold their bubbles and branches up into good paragraphs.

CUBING

What is cubing? Presented by Elizabeth Cowan Neeld in Writing, cubing is "a technique for swiftly considering a subject from six points of view. The emphasis is on swiftly and six" (21). Cubing gives writers a number of new ways to look at their subjects. This is where cubing works especially well--when a student may unable to look at a subject from more than one perspective.

To cube, students write from each of the six perspectives for three to five minutes each. When they have finished cubing, they have spent no more than thirty minutes on the exercise and have given themselves many more ways to look at their subject.

To cube as a prewriting activity, have your students respond to these six steps, which can be used to generate different points of view for any assignment (Cowan, 22):

1. Describe it. Using their senses, students look at the subject closely and describe it as vividly as possible.

2. Compare it/Contrast it. What is their subject like or not like?

3. Associate it. What comes to mind when they think about their subjects? Students associate the subject with something in their experience that is similar, that it reminds them of, that they've read about, that they've heard about, different times, places, people, events, etc.

4. Analyze it. Interpret the meaning of their topic, explaining its significance, telling how its made or put together.

5. Apply it. Have students tell what the subject does for their experience: what can they learn from it? How can it expand their knowledge, interests, understanding? Can it create a change in their perceptions of themselves and their worlds?

6. Argue for or against it. Students argue for the value, interest, importance of the subject. Why should someone else know about what they have to say? Students take a position and use any kind of reasons to support the position, even if they're illogical or silly.

As an individual discovery technique, cubing works well to get students out of a myopic rut. However, it also works well as a small group or paired exercise. Students look at one another's topics and respond to the six sides of the cube for one another. Students also can easily create a cube by folding their paper into six parts, using one part for each of the perspectives outlined above. There is more information about peer (or group) work in later inthis book.


TALK-WRITE

From a number of comments that I've made in the preceding examples of prewriting, you may have gotten the idea that talking can also be an extremely valuable prewriting activity. It is.

Where some students may have difficulty getting words on paper, even making a list, talking is the most natural activity that they routinely engage in--especially with their peers. Thus, giving students an opportunity to discuss their writing plans, problems, and ideas with other students or you, their instructor, gives them a greater chance to succeed in their pieces of writing.

Proposed by Robert Zoellner (1969) as talk-write, this prewriting (or for that matter, revising) technique is quite simple. Wixon and Wixon (1983) have this to say about talk-write:

It is simple and effective, gets students to help each other, makes writing social rather than solitary, allows for natural and positive discussion of the writing, and integrates language skills to the benefit of both speaking and writing (135).

To use talk-write, try some variation of Wixon and Wixon's exercise (129-130), such as the following:

1. Pair students up. Make certain they have pieces of blank paper.

2. Each person takes turns, once being the writer, once being the questioner.

3.  The writer talks out what he or she wants to say, while the questioner encourages the writer to keep talking. The questioner asks probing and open-ended questions such as "What happened next?" "I don't follow you. Can you say more about that?" "What was [the writer's subject] like? Or unlike? "

4.  Once the pair has plenty of ideas, the writer talks out his or her composition while the questioner writes it. The questioner helps the writer clarify, remember details and order. The questioner continues to ask relevant questions, help revise confusing details or references, and give positive feedback to the writer. The questioner should help without dominating.

5.  This initial finished piece will probably be messy from changing details, spelling, mechanics, etc. Once finished, the questioner should read the piece aloud so that the writer can hear the piece and make the necessary changes.

6.  Switch roles and repeat steps 1-5.

I particularly like to use talk-write when my students are writing a persuasive paper. When I do this, I have the students share their topics in groups of three, where one person takes notes while the other two exchange ideas in dialogue. Roles rotate, of course. The students engage in a Socratic-type of dialogue in the following way: Each student needs a clean piece of paper. On this he writes his thesis, followed by each of his major arguments both refuting his audience's objections and stating his own. Then, one by one, his partner's duty is to oppose each of the arguments. As she opposes the writer's points, a third person takes notes for the writer to have as helpful information in writing the argument. This works well as a prewriting activity after students have settled on a topic and their main objectives.

The preceding discussion of prewriting activities outlines some of the less structured activities, ones that help students to overcome the blank page, to make connections among new and old ideas, to discover details, and to examine a topic from a variety of perspectives. This discussion by no means exhausts all of the prewriting techniques that have been written about, but it does give you a flavor for a wide variety of possibilities. The next section of this chapter looks briefly at the more structured prewriting techniques.

## TEACHING STRUCTURED PREWRITING ACTIVITIES:  LIMITING THE SUBJECT AND LOCATING SUPPORTING DETAILS

Structured prewriting activities, most of them guided by a system of questions, provide the student with a tightly structured, step-by-step method for an intellectual probing of the student's subject. Unlike the unstructured, more intuitive discovery procedures, these structured prewriting activities work to guide a student through a deliberate analysis of an already determined subject.  These prewriting techniques, including classical invention's status (or stasis theory) and Topoi; Burke's Pentad; and Young, Becker, and Pike's particle, wave, and field analysis (or tagmemics), are extremely valuable for identifying and narrowing the thesis and discovering a variety of kinds of information--facts, ideas, feelings, beliefs, opinions, perspective--about the students' subjects.

## DEFINING THE THESIS: STASIS THEORY

In Classical Rhetoric for the Modern Student, 2nd ed., Corbett describes how students can use the classical rhetorical technique called "status" to define their thesis.  This procedure comes to us from the court system of ancient Rome where it was used to define what was at issue in a trial.  Classical rhetoricians, according to Corbett, "set up a useful formula for determining precisely the issue that was to be discussed" (150).  The thesis sentence, like the "status" of classical rhetoric, should present the student's precise issue.  It both defines the student's subject and asserts the student's stand, or point of view, on his subject.

The rhetoricians used a three-question formula for determining the exact issue of a trial or subject:

1.  An sit (whether a thing is) is a question of fact about the subject.  Students might consider asking themselves if the subject really exists, or if it really happened.  Corbett suggests asking questions about what evidence there is (examples, incidents, support), how reliable it is, if it is credible, and if there is conflicting evidence (Corbett, 150).

2.  Quid sit (what it is) is a question that calls for a definition of the essence of the subject.  Using specific details and facts, the student must define the boundaries of the subject.  Horner, in

Rhetoric in the Classical Tradition, recommends students'
asking questions such as "What is it?" "What is it like?" "Not
like?" and "What special terminology is associated with it?" to
explore the essence of the subject (32).

3.  Quale sit (of what kind it is) is a question that probes the
    quality of the subject. It involves questions of judgment such as
    "What are the consequences?" "Is it good or bad for me?" "For
    others?" "Is it right or wrong for me?" For others?" (Horner,
    32)

Having answered these questions, the student has a better idea
of what parts of the subject he wants to write about.  Next, he can
formulate his thesis.  For a complete discussion of status in Latin
rhetoric see Corbett, Classical Rhetoric for the Modern Student, 2nd ed.


DEVELOPING THE DISCOURSE: USING THE CLASSICAL TOPICS

Once your students have their subjects and have identified their
theses, they need to begin to explore the subject in order to develop
material.  The system of probing subjects that comes to us from such
classical rhetoricians as Aristotle and Quintillian, known as "topics," is
very useful.

The ancient rhetoricians, according to Corbett, developed the
system of topics as "an outgrowth of how the human mind thinks. . . .
The rhetoricians saw, for instance, that one of the tendencies of the
human mind is to seek out the nature of things.  So they set up the topic
of Definition.  Another tendency of the human mind is to compare
things, and when things are compared, one discovers similarities and
differences--and the differences will be in kind or in degree" (108).

Students might consider the following questions, which are an
adaptation of the common topics from classical rhetoric:

•   How would you define your subject for someone who knows
    less about it than you do?  Can you cite examples?  Incidents?
    Characteristics that make this subject different from others like
    it?

•   What is the nature of your subject?  What is it like?  Why?
    Unlike?  Why?  Is it more like or unlike some things than
    others?

- Has the subject caused something?  What has it been the effect of?  What comes before and after it?  Does some of the evidence contradict what you know?

- Consider it over time.  Under what circumstances is it possible or impossible?  What is its past like?  Its future?

- What support do you have for your thesis?  Have authorities spoken out about it?  Are there statistics?  What examples can you come up with to support your thesis?

## DEVELOPING THE DISCOURSE: LARSON'S CONTEMPORARY TOPICS

A modern application of Aristotle's topics engages the use of questioning as an exploratory means.  Richard L. Larson's system of questioning from "Discovery Through Questioning: A Plan for Teaching Rhetorical Invention" makes a case for teaching systematic invention in composition classes today.  Larson states:

> I propose therefore, that in our teaching of "invention" we make a persistent effort to force students to become as familiar as possible with the facts and possible relationships among the facts, about experiences on which they might write, and also that we force them to examine the facts underlying concepts they consider important and the content of propositions on which they may want to write. . . . I propose that students come to this through knowledge of their experiences, concepts, and propositions through a process of systematic questioning-- questioning which students engage in mostly by themselves, rather than questioning conducted by them for the teacher (147).

Larson (1975) poses a system of questions for a student to use as she explores her subject for supporting material.  An adaptation of this system follows:

- Students writing about some person, event, or object that exists in the present--a personal experience (Registering for college classes for the first time) or first hand observation (An observation of the local shopping mall) might ask questions that probe the physical characteristics of the subject: How is it different from or like other things? What is its structure? How is it put together and how do its parts work to make it a whole? Who needs it and why? What is its purpose? How would we evaluate it? Similarly, these questions can be asked of groups of items (Observations of a number of different shopping malls) like those above that occur in the present.

- <u>Students writing about something or group of things</u> that is either in the past or is on going--such as literature, history, personal experience, or observation--might ask questions that probe its happening: What happened, who did it, when, how, why, to whom. What circumstances surround the event? How was it like or unlike other events? What were its causes and consequences? Can it be evaluated and how?

- <u>Students writing about an abstract concept</u>, like democracy, might ask questions about its characteristics: How does the word connect with the student's experience? What characteristics does something need before it can qualify for this concept? How is it like or unlike other similar concepts (e.g., monarchy, socialism, anarchy)? Do you agree or disagree with all things subsumed by the concept? Why?

- <u>Students writing about a proposition</u>, taking a position on an issue that needs to be proved or disproved, such as "The college library should increase its weekend hours of operation," or The ozone layer is rapidly being depleted due to people's use of chemical aerosol sprays," might ask questions such as these: What must the reader know before he or she can be convinced? What key words are included and what do they mean in the context of the proposition? Can the student compare and contrast it with other propositions? How can it be illustrated? What kinds of evidence are available as support? Why might someone oppose it or not believe it? Does it make assumptions and does it have implications? Is what the student calls for feasible?

- <u>Students writing in response to questions</u> like, "Do automobile companies discriminate against young men who are under 25 years of age?" or "Should flag burning in the U. S. be prohibited by the Constitution?" might ask themselves questions like the following: When, in time does the question refer to? Present, past, or future? Why does the question arise and what are its assumptions? Is something fundamental in doubt? Can it be tested? Proven? Evaluated?

In answering these questions, students gather, sort, analyze, synthesize, and make judgments about their topics. Armed with a supply of such data, students can begin to solve their writing problems, having discovered ways to write about their observations and experiences and, through systems like this one, discovering and perfecting their ideas (Larson, 151-152).

## DEVELOPING THE DISCOURSE: BURKE'S PENTAD

Every journalist knows that to understand the whole, she must examine its parts, and thus she begins to analyze a story by asking the journalist's five questions: "who?" "what?" "when?" "where?" "why?" What is commonly known as Burke's Pentad is based on the same kind of questions, though Burke's are more closely aligned with literary criticism's dramatism. Easy to use and powerfully analytical, the Pentad applies the principles of drama to students' experiences, whether the students are studying literature or life. About the Pentad, Winterowd writes, "The Pentad . . . is an elegantly simple little set of probes, leading to obvious questions. . . . Complete answers to these questions will give anyone a fair survey of a work of drama, and also of any of the countless dramas of human history" (155).

The five key terms and their relative questions in Burke's Pentad are the following:

| | | |
|---|---|---|
| Act | -- | What took place in thought or deed? |
| Scene | -- | What is the background of the act or the situation in which it occurred? |
| Agent | -- | Who was involved? What person or kind of person performed the act? And were there co-agents or counteragents? |
| Agency | -- | How was the act accomplished? What means or instruments were used? |

Purpose --        Why did the act occur?

(adapted from Burke, A Grammar of Motives, xvii)

In addition to examining an experience through these five basic questions, students can also combine the five into ratios. For example, a student can manipulate the relationships by looking at the agent-agency, act-purpose, act-scene, ratios and so on.

## DEVELOPING THE DISCOURSE: PARTICLE, WAVE, FIELD ANALYSIS

Like classical invention and the Pentad, Young, Becker, and Pike's particle, wave, and field analysis is a structured system for the analysis of complex hierarchical systems, which Pike contends are basic to the human mind's functioning. About Pike's system, Tate writes, "Although it is impossible to prove that all complex systems are hierarchically structured, human beings appear to be incapable of understanding any other kind of system. The concept of hierarchy thus must be regarded as fundamental to any inquiry procedure" (33).

With this concept of hierarchy in mind, particle-wave-field analysis is designed to stimulate students' thinking about their topics in new ways. Winterowd writes about tagmemics:

Tagmemicists believe that in order for anyone to know a thing, three aspects of that thing's existence must be perceived: (1) how it differs from everything else [contrast], (2) how much it can change and still be itself [variation], and (3) how it fits into larger systems of which it is a part [distribution]. Tagmemic theory also tells us that we can view anything (concrete or abstract) from three perspectives: (1) as a particle, (2) as a wave, and (3) as a field. Taken together these six items obviously give us a nine-item heuristic (124).

Students, Pike says, can be taught to examine any subject from these angles. Thus, the particle aspect of a student's subject would be viewed from its contrast, variation, and distribution, as would the wave and field perspectives. These six characteristics--particle, wave, field, contrast, variation, distribution--form a nine-cell "tagmemic matrix" or grid from which to analyze a subject that a student is preparing to write about.   A complete example from a student' work writing about her "lavender rose" follows the description of the six perspectives.


### PARTICLE

If a student considers her subject first as a particle, she looks at it as the object, event, person, or place that is her topic, in terms of its visible and unchanging properties or characteristics, its apparent uniqueness.  "For purposes of analysis, you can take something apart to examine each piece or section of it, as if these pieces were the building blocks from which the object was created" (Memering and O'Hare, 56).

For example, if the student were considering a rose, she would identify its distinctive characteristics that make it the "thing" that it is.


### WAVE

Looking at the properties of the subject that make it unique, the particle aspect, is not enough.  Next, the student must consider her subject from the wave perspective.  In doing this, she examines it as part a larger group of things and looks at it to determine how much it can change before it is no longer a member of the class.  In doing this, she would be asking herself, "How was this thing created? What was the process that gave rise to its existence?"

In continuing to consider the rose, the student would look at it as something that is in process, that has grown from a root and may be harvested and sold.


### FIELD

Last, when she analyzes her subject as a field, she looks at it as a system itself (the parts that make up the whole) and also considers the subject as part of a larger system.

Last, the rose is itself a system whose parts work together to create the rose flower.  The rose can also be considered as part of a larger system or systems, such as the ecosystem, the system of weddings and funerals, and so on.

CONTRAST

Considering how her subject differs from subjects more or less like it is an important part of analyzing the subject. From each of the three perspectives, particle, wave, and field, she should consider "How is my subject different?"

How, the student now asks, is my rose different from other plants and flowers? Why is it a rose and not a daisy or a tomato?

VARIATION

She can also look at her subject as something that can possess variations but still exist as the object, event, person, and so on. How much change can it undergo before it is something else?

Next, she will ask about her rose, knowing that roses come in lots of sizes, shapes, colors, and varieties: "How much can this rose change before it can no longer be considered a rose?"

DISTRIBUTION

Last, your student looks at her subject and asks, "How is this a part of time and space?" From each of the three perspectives consider how your subject is distributed among objects, events, people, and whole systems like itself.

The student needs to consider how the rose fits into the larger systems of which it is a part. "How," she might ask, "is the rose affected by weather, by traditions, by consumerism, by landscaping?"

The following complete example demonstrates how a student could use particle-wave-field analysis to discover material to use in writing.

## MY LAVENDER ROSE

in contrast . . .

| Particle | Wave | Field |
|---|---|---|
| The rose I'm partial to is raspberry lavender. It's flower is small and delicate--about 1 inch i bloom. It's different from other roses on the bush because it's in perfect full bloom right now. Others are buds, tight and green, tight and lavender, hinting that they might open soon. Others are fading--brown tinged edges, petals falling to the ground. I'm particularly fond of this bush because my mother planted it for me, and we love it, because it reminds us of something else we love--black raspberry ice cream. | This single rose is dynamic--it's growing and changing all the time. It began as an idea to come, then became a real bud, now a flower, and soon to fade. Part of its dynamism is the pleasure it brings-- lovely to look at, wonderfully sweet to smell, warm memories it holds. I sit and look at it from my nearby chair where I drink my coffee and read the daily paper; I enjoy its brief but dynamic life. | This rose has many parts--a round little yellow center of pollen and things, hidden from my view right now. Many perfectly shaped, lavender rose petals, green leaves that support the petals from the base (what are they called?) The tall, not quite straight green stem that proudly holds up the flower. Many groups of leaves--each one consisting of 5-leaf clusters, radiating from a small branch, so rose-like. And prickers galore. All these parts work together like even largest most complex of systems to keep this rose healthy (or not). |

in variation . . .

Most people think roses are all pretty much the same. They're pretty, colorful, smell wonderful, make great bouquets and gifts. Roses are not a new craze--in fact Shakespeare wrote about them Despite many new"kinds" of flowers, roses are still the most popular, all-time favorite. Lots of people would like this rose because it's color is somewhat new--not the older traditional colors of red, pink, yellow, white. Unlike other flowers, roses have an odor that few flowers have. Even when they're dried. They also have lots of thorns--others do not.

This rose changes rapidly--if I pick it, it joins other flowers in a vase and helps to create a bouquet. I used to want to put it in a vase all by itself--it's so pretty. Now I sometimes put it in with otherflowers. They show one another off. The lavender rose always takes center stage though. Sometimes it gets dried and mixed into a batch of pot pourrie to make my drawer smell nice. Then it loses its lovely lavender color

early sun, and the night's droplets ofwatershimmer in the early light. It seems to almost sigh as it opens to the light. I think about picking it--that it could be in the house in a bouquet. It could even be in a wedding. For that matter, it could be dried and preserved forever as a memento of a special birthday. It could be squeezed into sweet-smelling rose water perfume, sold, and worn by someone else who loves roses.

in distribution . . .

The rose is part of my garden just outside my back door and to the immediate left. Beside this bush is another rose bush--not doing so well, but red. Also-- some marigolds and periwinkles happily in bloom in this garden with the swimming pool equipment humming beside them. The marigolds and the periwinkles don't get picked, so they stay there in the garden, where the rose is in constant danger of being whisked off.

This whole bush fits nicely into the garden. The lavender is such a subtle color splash among the whites and golds of the other flowers. This one also needs some food. It is like the cat who needs her Meow Mix, it won't flourish without its Miracle Grow on a regular basis. Its leaves turn brown, its flowers quietly quit, and it seems to say "I'm special and I deserve a treat." It's not like the rose growing on the trellis with lots of greenery and lots of tiny, tiny red flowers, that grows like a wild thing.

themselves--what's a wedding or a funeral if there are no roses? What's a Valentine's Day without the dozen long-stem roses from someone special? Roses symbolize entire systems of happiness, love, sympathy, congratulations, and friendship. They are often used to decorate parks, public gardens, medians, as well as residences because they are such show-offs.

Particle-wave-field analysis is a complex system for your students to use. You'll need to show them examples, work through examples in class, and be persistent. Like writing, this invention technique takes practice to understand and perfect.

## WORKS CITED Chapter 6

Aristotle. The Rhetoric of Aristotle. Trans. W. Rhys Roberts. New York: Random House, 1884.

Bardas, Mary Louise. "Writing For Understanding: The Self-Discovery Journal." A Letter from PALLA 3.1 (1989): 1,3.

Boley, Tommy J. SOAP Writing Assignments with Fine Art Transparencies. Austin, Texas: Holt, Rinehart and Winston, 1989.

Burke, Kenneth. A Grammar of Motives. Berkeley, CA: University of California Press, 1969.

---. A Rhetoric of Motives. Berkeley, CA: University of California Press, 1969.

Corbett, Edward P. J. Classical Rhetoric for the Modern Student, 2nd ed. New York: Oxford University Press, 1971.

Cowan, Elizabeth. Writing: Brief Edition. Glenview, Illinois: Scott, Foresman and Company, 1983.

Daniels, Harvey, and Steven Zemelman. A Writing Project: Training Teachers of Composition from Kindergarten to College. Portsmouth, New Hampshire: Heinemann Educational Books, Inc., 1985.

Elbow, Peter. Writing With Power. New York: Oxford University Press, 1981.

---. Writing Without Teachers. New York: Oxford University Press, 1973.

English, Hubert M., Jr. "Linguistic Theory as an Aid to Invention." College Composition and Communication 15 (1964): 136-40.

Flower, Linda. Problem-Solving Strategies for Writing, 2nd ed. New York: Harcourt Brace Jovanovich, 1985.

Fulwiler, Toby, ed. The Journal Book. Portsmouth, NH: Boynton/Cook Heinemann, 1987.

Graser, Elsa, R. Teaching Writing: A Process Approach. Dubuque, Iowa: Kendall/Hunt Publishing Company, 1983.

Harrington, David V. "Encouraging Honest Inquiry in Student Writing." College Composition and Communication 30 (1979): 182-86.

Horner, Winifred Bryan. Rhetoric in the Classical Tradition. New York: St. Martin's, 1988.

Irmscher, William F. Teaching Expository Writing. New York: Holt, Rinehart and Winston, 1979.

Lannon, John M. Technical Writing, 4th ed. Glenview, Illinois: Scott, Foresman/Little, Brown, 1988.

Larson, Richard M. "Discovery Through Questioning: A Plan for Teaching Rhetorical Invention." College English 30 (1968): (126-34).

Lindemann, Erika. A Rhetoric for Writing Teachers, 2nd ed. New York: Oxford University Press, 1987.

Memering, Dean, and Frank O'Hare. The Writer's Work. Englewood Cliffs, New Jersey: Prentice-Hall, Inc, 1980.

Murray, Donald M. "Write Before Writing." College Composition and Communication 29 (1978): 375-81.

Odell, Lee. "Measuring Changes in Intellectual Processes as One Dimension of Growth in Writing." Evaluating Writing: Describing, Measuring, Judging. Eds. Charles R. Cooper and Lee Odell. Urbana. Illinois: NCTE, 1977. 107-32.

---. "Piaget, Problem-Solving, and Freshman Composition." College Composition and Communication 24(1973): 36-42.

Pike, Kenneth L. "Beyond the Sentence." College Composition and Communication 15 (1964b), 129-35.

---. "A Linguistic Contribution to Composition." College Composition and Communication 15 (1964b): 82-88.

Rico, Gabriele Lusser. Writing the Natural Way. Los Angeles: J. P. Tarcher, Inc., 1983.

Wallace, Karl L. "Topoi and the Problem of Invention." Contemporary Rhetoric: A Conceptual Background with Readings. Ed. W. Ross Winterowd. New York: Harcourt Brace Jovanovich, Inc, 1975. 112-123.

Winterowd, W. Ross. Contemporary Rhetoric: A Conceptual Background with Readings. New York: Harcourt Brace Jovanovich, 1975.

Wixon, Vincent, and Patricia Wixon. "Using Talk-Write in the Classroom." Theory and Practice in the Teaching of Composition: Processing, Distancing, and Modeling. Eds. Miles Meyers and James Gray. Urbana, Illinois: NCTE, 1983. 129-35.

Young, Richard E. "Invention: A Topographical Survey." Teaching Composition: 10 Bibliographic Essays. Ed. Gary Tate. Fort Worth, Texas: Texas Christian University Press, 1976.

---, Alton L. Becker, and Kenneth L. Pike. Rhetoric: Discovery and Change. New York: Harcourt, Brace and World, 1970.

Zoellner, Robert. "Talk-Write: A Behavioral Pedagogy for Composition." Theory and Practice in the Teaching of Composition: Processing, Distancing, and Modeling. Eds. Miles Meyers and James Gray. Urbana, Illinois: NCTE, 1983. 122-28.

# CHAPTER 7:
# DRAFTING: THE ESSAY'S "OUTER SHAPE" AND "INNER PARTS"

The last chapter on prewriting was a real workout! The bonus comes now. If you and your students engage in a wide variety of prewriting strategies, the students will generate a large supply of ideas about their subjects--some useful and some not. They will have lots of material to work with. Having generated some potential content material and a generous supply of information about their subjects, students can now give it a form or some structure for a particular audience and purpose.

This chapter talks about ways to give that content material a structure so that the essay begins to say what the student wants it to say. To this end, this chapter about drafting is divided into two parts: "outer shape" and "inner parts" (Irmscher, 97). Outer shape refers to the structure of the essay as a whole, much as the exterior of your home has a shape. Inner parts refers to the sometimes visible, sometimes invisible techniques that contribute to making the paragraphs that hold the essay as a whole together, much like the wall boards, studs, and pipes contribute to the support and structure of your home.

About "outer shape" and "inner parts," William Irmscher says:

> The outer shape is the setting of limits that will define the whole--where the subject will begin, where it will end. . . . Paragraphing, however, is basic to the 'inner parts' . . . and to the ways those parts are fused to accomplish the qualities of unity and coherence that we usually associate with clear, readable writing (97).

This chapter about drafting will talk about how students look at their material to find an outer shape for the whole of the essay, and then, how they flesh that out by adding and developing paragraphs that will support that outer shape. Again, as with prewriting, the techniques for getting students to discover and create form vary
widely--from highly structured formulaic methods to pure discovery techniques. Their proponents span just as many decades as those who created and promoted the prewriting techniques, from Aristotle to the present.

The formulaic methods have both strengths and weaknesses. If a student has a formula at his fingertips, and is presented with a writing task, he can solve it: something akin to filling in the blanks. If he uses the five paragraph theme formula, for example, he knows that he needs an introduction, three main points, and a conclusion.  On the down side, formulas often    produce dreary, dull, lifeless prose that has little resemblance to how the writer is really thinking about his subject.

Unlike the formula-type of organizational scheme, allowing the content gathered during prewriting to suggest the organizational needs usually results in more interesting writing.  This approach is also more likely to achieve a result that reflects the writer's actual thoughts on his subject and that shapes the text in a way that the reader can follow easily.

In either case, now is the time to think, once again, very specifically about the audience and purpose for your students' essays.  Thinking about these two important issues helps students to weed through all the information that they have gathered in prewriting, selecting what bits and pieces of information they'll need both for the audience they have in mind and for the purpose they are trying to achieve.

The rest of this chapter discusses a variety of approaches to forming the outer shape and creating the inner parts.

## FORMING THE OUTER SHAPE

When you begin to have a student form an essay's outer shape, you have some choices about how to have them go about it. The shape of the whole essay determines its limits: the starting point where the writer makes promises, a middle ground where the writer fulfills those promises, and an ending point where the writer wraps up and reviews his promises.

## WHERE IT BEGINS: MAKING PROMISES

Two of the most important pieces of advice appear in many sources, including that of rhetorician Richard Whately: (1) Don't let students write long introductions.  The readers become impatient with the writer.  (2) Have students write their  introductions last.  ". . . an introduction that is composed last, will naturally spring out of the main subject, and appear appropriate to it" (Whately, 169).  With those two bits of advice in hand, we can move on to a more detailed look at introductions, how they work, and how they are composed.

Once your students begin to draft their essays, they are in the business of making promises to their readers. By putting the beginning or introductory words on the page, the writer is creating a relationship with her audience. In that relationship, the audience recognizes a set of expectations that are expected to be fulfilled. This is a good reason for having a solid introduction: if the audience recognizes expectations and they are different from the writer's, the communication is off to a bad start, one that will be difficult to fix.

According to Corbett (1990), the basic function of the introduction is to lead the audience into the piece of writing. He says that readers need to be eased into the discourse to prevent confusion.

The introduction, he says, has a two-fold purpose: (1) To orient the audience to the writer's reason for writing and (2) To create an atmosphere so that the audience will be receptive to what is being said (282). To orient the audience, students need to consider the nature of the subject since this influences the choices for introductory material. As writers, students practice arousing their audience's interest or curiosity.

In writing their introductions, students will need to address a number of variables as they consider their audience and how much the audience knows: Do they need to show how the subject is important or momentous or is that evident? Will they need to show how the topic is relevant to the audience and their interests? Will they need to show how their subject is pleasant or startling (Corbett, 283)?

There are times, of course, when arousing interest in the subject is not a top priority. The subject may have intrinsic interest for the audience (e.g., a discussion of cold fission for the University Physics Newsletter), or the circumstances may make it interesting (e.g., the inaugural address given by the President of the U. S.). Most times, though, the writer cannot depend on capturing the audience. In these cases, she needs to write what some people (e.g., Zinsser) call a "hook" to get the audience's interest and to orient them to her reasons for writing.

The second job of the introduction is to create the kind of tone that will make the audience open to what is being said. Corbett calls this "ingratiating oneself with the audience." The writer needs to establish some credibility for herself so that the audience knows that she is qualified to write about the topic. Corbett says that the writer needs to exercise "due restraint and becoming humility" (288).

Practically speaking, you may be wondering what all this means. When a student writes an introduction, she needs to announce the topic and state the thesis early to get the reader's attention. When the topic is announced, the student might move from a general statement to a more specific statement in the introduction.

For example, the student's introduction that follows begins with a question about success in college that draws the reader into the context from which the writer writes. Next, the student narrows the topic and forms her thesis statement. Last, the student composes an organizational statement that guides her writing and the reader's reading.

> Why are some students more successful in college than others? My guess is, after one semester of college, that it has a lot to do with their study habits. In fact, I believe that hearing about some good study techniques will nearly guarantee your success as a college student. My advice is: budget your time, read and revise your class notes right after class, and talk to other students about the class.

The student in this example uses a question to get the audience's attention. While this is one effective way to begin, Corbett (using Whately) describes five basic ways to beginning as essay:

1. Introduction inquisitive. "to show that our subject is important, curious, or interesting" (282).

2. Introduction paradoxical. "to show that although the points we are trying to establish seem improbable, they must after all be admitted" (284).

3. Introduction corrective. "to show that our subject has been neglected, misunderstood, or misrepresented" (284).

4. Introduction preparatory. "to explain an unusual mode of developing our subject; or to forestall some misconception of our purpose; or to apologize for some deficiencies" (285).

5. Introductive narrative. "to rouse interest in our subject by adopting the anecdotal lead-in" (286).

Students get the hang of writing and recognizing good introductions fairly quickly. The following exercises work well when you want students to practice constructing the beginnings to their essays. Studying SAMPLE beginnings and talking about them is a good way to get students to look at what works and how it works. You can have them bring in the beginning paragraphs from an article, essay, or story. Or if you use a reader, you can select beginning paragraphs from readings. Have the students look at these paragraphs as readers (either individually or in small groups of three or four) asking the following questions: What would the reader's expectations be for the rest of the piece of writing? How do you think that the writer will fulfill those expectations? What are the cues that point out these features of the beginning to you as a reader, i. e., what words indicate who the audience is and what the purpose of the essay is? What other choices did the writer have?   Last, you might ask the students to rewrite these paragraphs for a different audience and purpose.

SCRAMBLED paragraphs work well for a close look at the differences that organization can make in an individual paragraph. Prepare a handout with the sentences from paragraphs listed out of order. Have students, again either individually or in small groups, put the paragraph together. Have them describe and defend their order. You might have overhead transparency film available for them to prepare the paragraphs on, so they can then show them to the class as they talk about them. The point you want to make is that there is no single possible order, but there may be a best one. Discuss the differences in emphasis that are created by the differences in organization. If the group agrees that there is a best way to organize the paragraph, discuss why that is so.

The next part of this chapter talks about how students fulfill the promises that they make in their beginning paragraphs. You'll see that there are a number of ways to approach the overall outer shape of the piece of writing. Some of these are formulaic; others are not.


## WHERE IT GOES: FULFILLING PROMISES

Creating the middle, where the writer fulfills the beginning's promises usually gets tackled first, before the students write their beginnings, but after they have their basic thesis in mind. The following will introduce you to a variety of ways to have students write the middle or body portion of their essays.

Formula or not?   A formula for overall development of the outer shape can be useful for a student, especially one who is having a difficult time getting words on paper. In this way, a formula serves as a springboard to other possibilities. Some people believe that if students learn to organize a piece of writing first with a formula, they have a schema to work from and later they can spring from that to discover other methods of organization. This is not much different from an architect, who uses a basic blueprint to get started, but as he becomes more skilled at designing, he varies the blueprint to make more interesting and creative home designs. Like the builder, the students who are not yet ready to allow their thoughts to shape themselves on paper have an essay-writing blueprint that works to shape the content, and they are able to build a piece of writing.


### THE FIVE-PART APPROACH

The five-part (often called the five-paragraph theme) approach is an old standard, coming to us directly from Aristotle, Cicero, and Quintillian, among other classical rhetoricians. This approach to the outer shape of a piece of writing assumes that all discourse has three main points. Consequently, the finished product has an introduction, a three-part middle, and a conclusion.

The <u>beginning</u> is usually funnel-shaped when diagrammed visually (Baker). This means that the essay opens with a generalization that sets the context or broad topic area for the writing. Next, it moves to a specific statement about the topic, usually the thesis statement. Last, the opening concludes with an organizational statement that identifies the three main points to be developed in the order in which they will be developed. The previous example introduction adheres to this funnel-shaped pattern. The beginning can be a single paragraph or more depending upon the finished length of the piece of writing; for example, a book may have one entire chapter devoted to the introduction.

The <u>middle</u> of the essay that is constructed using the five-part approach develops each of the three main points. This can mean one paragraph per point, but it can also mean several paragraphs per point.

The <u>conclusion</u> of the essay, like the introduction, may be one paragraph, but it can also be more. The conclusion if diagrammed visually, looks like an inverted funnel (Baker). This means that the most specific point comes first, generally a summation of the three main points, followed by a restatement of the thesis, and winding up with a broad generalization about the topic.

Each of the five parts of classical discourse thus performs a specific function. Corbett (1990) summarizes the five-parts of classical discourse in the following manner:

1.  <u>Introduction</u> that introduces the writer's purpose and point of view to the audience;

2.  <u>Statement of the facts or circumstances</u> about the subject that the reader needs to know;

3.  <u>Points</u> that <u>support</u> the writer's thesis;

4.  <u>Points</u> that <u>refute</u> the opposing point of view;

5.  <u>Conclusion</u> that brings together the main points, restates the thesis, and shows the significance of the point (25, 282-316).

Young, Becker, and Pike offer a similar, but essentially four-part arrangement for the essay (especially the persuasive essay). They advise using the following superstructure for the essay's outer shape:

1.  Introduction to the topic;

2.  Background to the issue being written about;

3.  The argument itself which includes four elements:

    - a major premise (a stated generalization, the most often quoted example of which is "All men are mortal"),

    - the minor premise (a particular example that supports the generalization, "Socrates is a man"),

    - the conclusions (what follows from these two statements, "Therefore Socrates is mortal"), and

    - the superiority of the position being presented over alternative positions;

4.  Conclusion which includes a summary of the thesis and a final statement about its importance (234-5).

They advise students to vary this basic strategy based on what the readers' perspectives are likely to be.

"WRITING TO THE POINT"

"Writing to the point" is a system for developing hierarchically arranged ideas that was advocated by William J. Kerrigan and Allan A. Metcalf in Writing to the Point. He saw this system as an indispensable one for helping students to develop clear, unified prose, using specific and concrete details. The system is a tightly organized one that uses the following six essential steps (Kerrigan and Metcalf):

1.  "Write a short, simple, declarative sentence that makes one statement."   Kerrigan and Metcalf advise making a definite statement, not a question or a command.   They advance the following formula for creating this statement (4-6):

    SOMEONE IS/WAS SOMETHING.
    SOMETHING DOES/DID SOMETHING.

    E.g., "My third grade teacher, Mr. Holmes, had an important influence on my life."

2.  "Write three sentences about the sentence in Step 1--clearly and directly about the whole of that sentence, not just something in it" (18).

    E.g., He taught me the importance of not making fun of others.
    He taught me that I am a uniquely special person.
    He showed me that learning is fun.

3.  "Write four or five sentences about each of the three sentences in Step 2--clearly and directly about the whole of the Step 2 sentence, not just something in it" (31).

4.  "Make the material in the four or five sentences in Step 3 as specific and concrete as possible.  Go into detail.  Use examples.  Don't ask, 'What will I say next?'  Instead, say some more about what you have just said.  Your goal is to say a lot about a little, not a little about a lot" (43-44).

5.  "In the first sentence of each new paragraph, starting with Paragraph 2, insert a clear reference to the idea of the preceding paragraph" (105).

6. "Make sure every sentence in your theme is connected with, and makes a clear reference to, the preceding sentence" (123).

In advocating this system for writing essays, Kerrigan and Metcalf point out that steps 1, 2, and 3 get students writing around a unified point. Step 4 builds in the specificity of using concrete details, and Steps 5 and 6 provide the coherence that their essays need.

Kerrigan and Metcalf also recommend that steps may also be repeated. For example, they advise that after Step 4, students take a break and look at the grammar a bit, do some reading, and think about their readers. This break gives the students a chance to look to outside reading as a guide to developing style and to look carefully at what they are writing and why.

They advise, further, that students repeat Step 4 before moving on to Step 5 and that they review Step 1 after completing Step 5. While this, like the preceding systems is a rigid, formulaic system, students who need assistance getting their words on paper may find this appealing for awhile. Be certain though that they realize that all good prose is not necessarily constructed according to such strict formulas and that they too will move on to the discovery of their own form based on their subject material.

## THE RHETORICAL MODES

A standard approach to the teaching of composition for many years was the rhetorical modes approach. This meant that students wrote essays whose outer shape was fashioned by a single strategy such as description, comparison and contrast, classification, process analysis, and definition. D'Angelo (1975; 1985) defends this approach by saying that these paradigms reflect the mind's thought processes. Lindemann interprets D'Angelo as saying that there is a "close connection between invention and arrangement, between thought processes and the organizational patterns or paradigms that express ideas" (Lindemann, 166). These paradigms are like maps, D'Angelo says, and in this way have value. They allow the writer to move his or her "thinking in an orderly manner from the beginning of an essay to its conclusion" (Process, 53).

D'Angelo divides the rhetorical modes into two groups because he believes that as the writer composes, the material is put into patterns of time, space, or logic. Consequently, he divides these modes into a "static" group (patterns that are fixed in time and space) and a "progressive" group (patterns that move through time and space or are dynamic). The following are some of the commonly used modes in freshman English, including their suggested patterns of development.

Description. Generally a student writes a descriptive essay early in the term and he is writing about personal experience to express his view of his real world. When a student writes a descriptive essay, he investigates something in great detail: an object, a person, a place. To do this, he must move systematically over the object of description, often engaging all five of his senses (sight, hearing, taste, smell, touch). Description also includes a close physical examination of the subject. So, for example, to write thoroughly about the subject from a physical perspective, the student must move from top to bottom, or bottom to top; he must move from left to right, or right to left; move from inside to outside; or move in a clockwise order.

Comparison and Contrast. Because comparison and contrast are skills basic to everything people do in life, having students look for the similarities and differences between two or more items puts them in touch with ways of evaluating what people say, what kind of things to purchase (brand of computer, for example), and what they think about issues in general. To write an essay that is pure comparison and contrast, the student writes an introduction that sets up the thesis and the comparison; the student also writes a conclusion that clinches the differences or similarities and makes the point. The middle portion must adhere to one of the following organizational patterns:

> Subjects' Pattern: In this scheme, the author talks about each item in a separate part of the essay. Under each item, he discusses the characteristics that he is comparing and contrasting. For example, in writing about city life and country life, the student would write about city life first. Under that subject, he would include the characteristics, such as amount of crime, quality of schools, open spaces. Then, he would talk about the same characteristics only under the subject of country living.

> Characteristics' Pattern: In this pattern, the writer would take up the characteristics individually. Thus, he would write about the amount of crime, discussing first city life, then country life, and so on.

Classification.    In their daily lives, students are constantly putting things, events, and people into groups that are alike. Because this too seems like a natural activity of the mind, understanding this kind of cataloguing can be useful to students in making their points clear for their readers.

When they write classification essays, students divide their subject into chunks or categories to help readers understand the subject better.  In the end, the overall organizational pattern is the following: introduction with thesis; group 1, group 2, group 3; and a conclusion that makes the point of the classification.  Significant classification systems help the reader to understand the subject better or in a new way. For example, a student writing to a student audience describing differing demands of university professors divided them into these three groups: the "he-thinks-this-class-is-my-life" professor, the "she-treats-us-like-bimbos" professor, and the "she-understands-I-have-a-brain-and-a-life" professor.

Process Explanation.    A process paper gives directions for how someone will complete some process. It is a "how to" paper; it tells the reader, for example, how to change a tire, how to bake a cake, how to register for classes.  The organizational pattern breaks the process down into its component stages and looks generally like this: the introduction (This includes a statement of purpose and an organizational statement; it may also include a list of materials.); step 1; step 2; step 3, and so on; a conclusion (that summarizes the results of the process).

Definition.    When students write definition papers, they are attempting to define what a concept or an idea means.  This is a useful technique in learning how differently people think about the same concept, for example, about "freedom."  To develop a definition paper, students should use an organizational plan that includes the following: introduction (including a sentence definition and a plan for the paper); subsequent sections can be developed by using an illustration, examples, contrast with other similar concepts; and a conclusion that makes the point of the essay.

These five modes of development--description, comparison and contrast, classification, process explanation, and definition--are the ones most commonly used for Freshman English.  Of these modes, D'Angelo would place description, definition, classification, and comparison in the static paradigm and  process explanation in the progressive paradigm.

If you opt for this organizing principle for teaching Freshman Composition, I'd give you one strong word of caution to pass on to your students: When they have finished writing their essays, have them answer the question, "So what?" Because this pure modes approach can lead to hollow prose with no purpose, this questioning ("So What?") is an important safeguard against writing to the product only. If they can answer this question about their own or another student's essay, they have succeeded in making a point.

While, like the contemporary five-part essay, these systems seem mechanical, all three approaches--the five-part essay, writing to the point, and the rhetorical modes--give inexperienced writers some often badly needed guidance with organization. They do, however, in their rigidity, divorce the form from the content. Consequently, as teachers, we need also to recognize the importance of discovery in the shaping of form and teach it to our students too. Larson puts it this way:

> The planning of any piece of writing thus involves much more than the replication of a previously discerned pattern of discourse. It requires the choice of an order specially tailored to the subject, to the writer's view of that subject, to the goal sought by the writer, to the reader(s), and to the situation within which it will be perceived (Structure, 60).

## DISCOVERING THE SHAPE: BLOCKING

Blocking (Lindemann, 1987), in direct contrast to all of the previous means to create the outer shape of an essay, asks students to discover the shape that best supports the content they have accumulated for their essay, the audience for whom they are writing it, and the aim or purpose they intend to achieve. With this in mind, let's look closely at blocking.

Blocking is a fairly unstructured and visual way for students to plan what their intentions for their essays are. "Blocking asks students to draw a picture of what they propose to write. Guided by questions they ask of their material, their audience, and their purpose, they fill in their drawing one layer at a time" (Lindemann, 163). They move back and forth between the material they have gathered during the prewriting period, selecting material to fill in the blocks that they have decided they will need for their essays. Blocks can eventually get subdivided, deleted, moved around, and elaborated upon.

Lindemann describes blocking in this way:

> Blocking helps students shape their writing by looking simultaneously at their materials and at the expectations of an audience. . . . The paper is likely to be more effective because the writer has taken the time to review prewriting decisions, creating a visual representation of how the inner parts work and the outer shape of the piece might work together to convey a message to a reader (165).

Lindemann suggests that students ask themselves questions like these: "How many blocks will I need?" and "What should each block do?"

After getting some blocks of material on paper, students need to ask themselves: "What order will get my audience through the essay best?" "How much space will each block of information take up?" "How will I develop each block?"

Once students get to the "How" questions, they have switched the focus away from what they are saying, the information itself, to how they will say it, the rhetorical strategies they'll use to target the intended audience and purpose.

When they are finished, the students have a visual representation of what they are going to say.

Lindemann recommends that you give students a handout with questions to guide their blocking. Try the following, or some like them:

1. What do I know about [my subject]?

2. What does [my audience] want to know about [my subject]?

3. How many blocks of material will I need?

4. What job is each block supposed to do?

5. What material goes into each block? Move material from prewriting to the blocks. Create sub-blocks if it seems like a good idea.

6. What order would best help my audience read my essay?

7. How much space, roughly, do I want each block to take up?

8. How do I want to develop each block?

9.  Share your blocks with other members of the class and get feedback.

Because of its loosely structured nature, students will probably need your help and their classmates' help in learning to block their papers. The questions above provide useful guidance for  conferences with you and with other members of the class.


## WHERE IT ENDS: WRAPPING UP PROMISES

The conclusion to the essay wraps up the loose ends, restates the significant promises you have made. It can, like the other parts of the essay, be written by adhering to a formula.

If you want to offer your students a formula for writing the conclusion, tell them to picture the concluding remarks as if they formed an inverted funnel, moving from the most specific statement to a broad generalization.  Their first sentence should be the most specific, summarizing the main points of the essay. Next, restate the thesis, and last, make a general concluding statement that wraps up the discussion. Often, teachers ask students to end with a startling fact, quote, or piece of information or advice.

Returning to the example of the "studying in college" essay, the conclusion that follows adheres to this inverted funnel plan:

> You can see how using your time wisely, working with your class notes immediately, and building class information into conversation can enhance your chances for success in college. Having gotten my advice for succeeding in college, I hope you'll consider it seriously. I, too, used to think studying was only for nerds!

Regardless of the formula, the wrap up should close the discussion without leaving any doubt in the reader's mind that the essay is over. Like the introduction, it need not be long.

Having looked at a number of possibilities for handling the outer shape of the essay, next we'll look at a variety of approaches to creating the inner parts.

## CREATING THE INNER PARTS

You've gotten your students through the initial stages of planning their essays. Whatever approach you've taken to having them formulate a blueprint for the outer shape of their essays, you're ready to guide them one step further: creating the inner parts that will hold that outer shape together. They know what they want to say based on their plans for the outer shape; now it's time to address how to say it.

Much like your guidance when the students form the outer shapes of their essays, you also have an essential choice for guiding your students through this stage of drafting their essays: the discovery approach or the formulaic approach to filling in the text.

Knowing what a good paragraph looks like and reads like is not the same as writing a decent paragraph. We often tell our students that their paragraphs need to demonstrate three main qualities: emphasis, coherence, and unity. To this we often have added that they ought to be three to five sentences long, that we indent at beginning of each one, and that the ideas in the paragraph ought to show relationships among the ideas--i. e., subordination and/or coordination of ideas. This all makes perfect sense when we (teacher and students) have a paragraph product to analyze.

But when we sit down to write the paragraph, these noble ideas give us little help in actually constructing the paragraph. About this, Lindemann says, "Instead of focusing instruction on what paragraphs are, we need to teach students how to discover relationships and express them in units of discourse. To be sure, it's much easier to teach students 'about' paragraphs, isolating the shapes and labels, but if we want them to 'do' paragraphs, we must teach not paragraphs but paragraphing" (146).

## PARAGRAPH DEVELOPMENT: MODES AS METHOD

Developing paragraphs according to the mode that they express is an old standby, and one that is in wide use today. This includes such development patterns as description, narration, definition, classification and division, example, comparison and contrast, analogy, process analysis, cause and/or effect, enumeration, and illustration. The most sophisticated pattern is a combination of the above.

A student might use a variety of these patterns within an essay. For example, she might have blocked an essay about a traffic accident that she was involved in.  In her block, she might identify paragraphs such as these:

- How did it happen (process)?

- How did I feel (descriptive)?

- What did my car look like (descriptive)?

- What did the other car look like (comparison)?

- What did I tell my parents (narrative)?

- What effects will this have on my life (cause-effect)?

Having made these decisions, the student can then begin to decide how much space each of these parts will occupy and to arrange them in an order that will make her point clear to her audience.

In a somewhat different vein, Becker (1965), maintains that there are only two basic paragraph patterns that students can be taught to generate: topic, restriction/expansion, illustration (TRI/IRT); and problem/solution (PS) or question/answer (QA) (Becker, 1965).

In the first pattern, which Becker calls the TRI pattern, students present their topics as propositions.  These propositions should state or imply relationships such as comparison, contrast or classification.  Next, the topic is restated by its being restricted and made more specific.  Last, examples, analogies, and the like elaborate upon the point.  This pattern creates what is commonly known as a deductive paragraph.  If this pattern is reversed (IRT), an inductive paragraph is created.  Becker says it is also possible to have this pattern without the restrictive element, having just the TI.

The second pattern, which Becker calls the problem/solution pattern (PS), can also take the form of a question/answer (QA).  In this pattern, the problem is stated often in question form or as an effect which is going to be explained.  Next, the solution or cause is discussed.  Often, he says, the solution section may be shaped using a TRI structure.

In either pattern, each of the elements can be filled by one or more sentences, but Becker claims that a paragraph can reach closure for the reader only when the pattern is completed.

## PARAGRAPH DEVELOPMENT: GENERATING PARAGRAPHS

A number of people have written about discovering or generating paragraphs rather than constructing them.  Rodgers, for example, says that writers intuitively know where to paragraph, when they are at the end of a paragraph.  In "The Stadium of Discourse," he says that paragraph indentations are for reader's interpretation only.  A student places new paragraphs based on how he or she wants the reader to interpret as she reads.  For example, if your students tend to write long paragraphs, a short one provides some contrast or can be used to emphasize the point.  Alternatively, if students are writing short paragraphs, a long one produces a reflective tone when added to the structure.

Knowing that the structure of the inner parts affects the reader's interpretation, Rodgers recommends that students paragraph with this in mind.  Consequently, a student should think about whether to write one paragraph that is long or to divide it into two or three, based more on the way she wants her audience to interpret her ideas.

Irmscher (1975) talks about intuitive paragraphing in these words:

> What experiments with paragraphing inevitably confirm is an intuitive perception of paragraph patterns that can be separated or combined in various ways. . . . A bloc of four paragraphs might very well have one topic sentence that embraces the bloc of four as a whole.  Thus, the paragraphing a writer chooses may be only one way--that writer's way--of partitioning the material.  It is helpful to have students consider alternative paragraphing, for then they begin to realize what paragraphs do, how the structural divisions can affect the interpretation of a passage (101).

Last, and probably the most used and useful, the Christensen method explains how to use generative paragraphing.  He says that a paragraph is a "sequence of structurally related sentences" (25).  By this he means that people intuitively write paragraphs that are hierarchical in nature, that there is an intrinsic relationship that exists in the levels of generality, addressed by sentences within a paragraph (or paragraphs within an essay).

The topic sentence is the most general in the paragraph, written at the highest level of generality.  Subsequent sentences are written at lower levels of generality, or to say it in another way, are more specific than the topic sentence. Within a single paragraph, then, sentences operate at various levels, coordinating with one another or subordinating one to another.

Writing, Christensen indicates, proceeds on the basis of generality and particularity, and moves back and forth between levels of generality. Writers, he contends, are always striving to make themselves clear and do this by being increasingly more specific as they explain their points. In talking about using the Christensen method, Irmscher says, "Our sense of incompleteness in an essay is frequently due to a lack of balance between the generalizations and the particulars. The thought may be complete, but not the structure" (103).

Christensen recommends having students look at existing paragraphs of their own or of published writers for this structure. By examining the work of published writers, students can then imitate the paragraphs in their own writing.

Paragraphing is basic to creating an essay's inner parts and to the way in which those inner parts come together to achieve the goals of emphasis, unity, and coherence. As Lindemann reminds us, prewriting often suggests a form for the piece of writing. Also, "as we probe the subject to discover what we want to say, as we define our purposes and assess the expectations of our audience, we make choices which ultimately are reflected in the organization of the written work. A subject probed thoroughly enough begins to organize itself, begins to suggest possibilities for arranging its presentation" (159).

There is a dissonance that many teachers, especially new teachers, feel in trusting to your students' intuition as they create essays; but in so doing, you free them to write what they want to say, not what they think you want to hear. In doing that, you stretch their thinking and their intellectual abilities and do them a real educational service.

WORKS CITED Chapter 7

Baker, Sheridan. The Practical Stylist. 5th ed. New York: Harper and Row, 1982.

Becker, Alton L. "A Tagmemic Approach to Paragraph Analysis." College Composition and Communication 16 (1965): 237-242.

Christensen, Francis. "A Generative Rhetoric of the Paragraph." Rhetoric and Composition: A Sourcebook for Teachers. Ed. Richard L. Graves. Rochelle Park, New Jersey: 1976. 162-178.

Corbett, Edward P. J. Classical Rhetoric for the Modern Student. 3rd ed. New York: Oxford University Press, 1990.

D'Angelo, Frank. Process and Thought in Composition. 3rd ed. Boston: Little, Brown, 1985.

Irmscher, William F. Teaching Expository Writing. New York: Holt, Rinehart and Winston, 1979.

Kerrigan, William J. and Allan A. Metcalf. Writing to the Point. 4th ed. San Diego: Harcourt, Brace, Jovanovich, Publishers, 1987.

Larson, Richard L. "Structure and Form in Non-fiction Prose." Teaching Composition: 10 Bibliographic Essays. Ed. Gary Tate. Fort Worth, Texas: Texas Christian University Press, 1976. 45-72.

Lindemann, Erika. A Rhetoric for Writing Teachers. 2nd ed. New York: Oxford University Press, 1987.

Rodgers, Paul. "The Stadium of Discourse." Rhetoric and Composition: A Sourcebook for Teachers. Ed. Richard L. Graves. Rochelle Park, New Jersey: 1976. 179-182.

Whately, Richard. Elements of Rhetoric. Ed. Douglas Ehninger. Carbondale, Illinois: Southern Illinois University Press, 1985.

Young, Richard E., Alton L. Becker, and Kenneth L. Pike. Rhetoric: Discovery and Change. New York: Harcourt, Brace and World, 1970.

# CHAPTER 8:
# REWRITING--REVISING

Why do many students resist revising? Is it that they don't know that most writers do rewrite and revise regularly? Is it that they have had teachers who seldom praised their work? Is it that they believe that once it's written, it's done--once on paper it's finished, so don't mess it up? What does rewriting suggest to our students? Rewriting is the subject of Chapters 8 and 9 of this book.

What is rewriting? To some it could mean "write again." In a sense that interpretation is true, but it doesn't necessarily mean "begin from scratch." In the context of students' writing, rewriting has two main possibilities, both equally important to them finishing a piece of writing. On one hand, rewriting means revision, reviewing what has been written for internal qualities--especially content and organization. In doing this, students often need readers to help them determine if what they have written will achieve their purpose as authors and will be clear to their audience as readers. This part of rewriting is called revision because, in keeping with the Latin roots of the word, it means to "see again," to take another look. Sometimes revision requires that the writer do little to change the text; other times, revision requires the writer to change the text significantly.

In addition, rewriting can also mean editing or proofreading. Once a student has all the ideas in place, all the details selected, all the sentences and paragraphs in the proper order, then, and only then, does it make sense to polish the surface. That means that all the grammar, spelling, and punctuation changes often can occur last. Imagine a student searching for the right spelling, the best punctuation, before she has fully decided to keep that part of her draft for her final paper, only to decide to throw away some of what she has written. What a waste of a writer's time, to have emphasized surface features at a time in the writing process when other things--chiefly content--should have been the focus! So, hard as it can be for you as the teacher, reserve commenting upon the surface features until toward the end of the process. Remember that you wouldn't paint the wallboard before you put it up.

It is true that not every one of your students needs to revise everything that gets written, but it is also true that every one of them needs to know what rewriting means, what it entails, how to go about it, and how its two aspects of revision and editing/proofreading differ. This chapter talks about revision as part of rewriting; the next chapter talks about editing as part of rewriting.

Revision as rewriting really means testing--testing the writing to see if it works, like testing the gas grill after putting it together. When students test their writing, they are checking to see if their purpose has been accomplished and if their audience has been reached. This phase allows students a chance to adjust the content and the organization to make it all work better, more effectively, more efficiently.

As teachers, we can encourage students to revise in two ways: through conferencing with them ourselves and by having them read one another's work in response groups.

## CONFERENCING WITH STUDENTS

"Conferences, opportunities for highly productive dialogues between writers and teacher-readers," says Muriel Harris, "are or should be an integral part of teaching writing" (3). By engaging students in one-on-one discussion of their own writing, we have the opportunity to put writing in a very personal perspective, one that points to a specific writer's strengths, weaknesses, and concerns.

While some teachers use conferencing as one step in the teaching of writing, some do not use conferencing at all, and some use conferencing almost exclusively.    Emig (1960) describes how conferences can be integrated in high school writing instruction; Carnicelli (1980) uses conferences as an additional ingredient in teaching college writing, Murray (1982) says to have short and frequent conferences with a clear focus, and Garrison (1974) dispenses with classroom instruction in favor of teaching entirely through the conference method.    Whatever strategy you choose for including conferencing in your writing instruction, knowing how conferencing can fit in, what it can do for your students' writing, and some do's and don'ts help to understand conferencing as a possible ingredient in your instruction package.

## HOW DOES CONFERENCING FIT IN?

One of the most important accomplishments of conferencing is that students talk specifically and concretely about their own writing and about themselves as writers.    Writing instruction in this setting is no longer abstract and non-specific, since you are sitting side-by-side talking about the individual student's specific piece of writing. For you, the end result should be that final drafts are easier to read and grade, since you will have seen where the writing began, how it moved, the changes that were made, and how it got where it is.

You can decide how conferencing fits into your classroom instruction. If, as Garrison recommends, you choose to conduct your class almost entirely through conferencing, your classroom takes on a daily workshop environment. Students come prepared to work on a writing project and to talk with you about their work-in-progress. As the teacher, you spend a very brief period of time with individual students for the entire period. This means as little as two to three minutes per student. Garrison found that he could often talk to twenty students in a single class period of fifty minutes (reported in Carnicelli, 104). In this format, each conference is devoted to one or two very specific issues in a student's writing, such as point of view in one paragraph or the kind of elaboration used to make a single point.

Many of us enjoy the classroom interaction and genuinely believe that we have important information to give to students, in which case this Garrison method does not suit our teaching styles. Carnicelli (1980) recommends conferencing in addition to regular classroom teaching. Often, teachers have conferences in place of a single class meeting. This change in routine provides students with a class period during which they can go to the library, seek a classmate's advice, or work on their writing, while the teacher devotes several hours in his or her office to meeting with individual students and discussing their writing.

If you opt to conference, and to use the system that Carnicelli (among others) recommends, schedule your time carefully. Have students sign up for a specific time to come to your office to discuss their writing. Arrange the students at regular intervals of ten, fifteen, twenty, or more minutes. Think about your own interaction style when you think about how long the conference should be. If you are likely to want or need time for some casual talk, build it into the conference time. Don't let students queue up outside your door because you've gotten behind. Allow yourself a couple of breaks during this extended conference time, too. Many hours of continuous conferencing can be very tiring.

Set an agenda for the conference. In deciding what to talk about in a writing conference, you must make some choices--set priorities since you can't talk about everything. The first thing you have to decide is whether to read the paper before the conference or during the conference. Some people have found that they can read during the conference and give useful feedback. On the other hand, Carnicelli's study (1980) showed that students felt that they got better feedback if the teacher had read the paper before the conference.

If you have read the students' papers before the conference, make notes to yourself about the kinds of questions you'll ask the student.   Both Garrison and Carnicelli recommend thinking about students' writing in this order: content, point of view, organization, style, and mechanics (103).   To decide what you and the student will talk about during the conference, for example, look first at the content of the student's paper.  If this seems adequate, look to the student's point of view, and so on, keeping in mind that not every draft needs to be substantially revised, nor do all drafts even need formal conferencing.

Some teachers ask that students guide the conference by coming prepared with questions to ask or concerns that they have about the writing that they are doing.  This further puts the responsibility for revision on the student; moreover, it takes the focus off the teacher as evaluator, and places the focus on the teacher as reader.

Whatever your approach to the conference time, be focused, and insist that your students arrive focused too, because if you're not, you'll both waste valuable time.

Another thing to think about is how many conferences to have for each paper.  Some teachers like to have more than one conference, including one to talk about the student's plans for the paper.  Others have conferences only when the students have completed a rough draft.

Last, think about the kinds of students you could have--from passive to indifferent to hostile to talkative to unprepared.  Each of these cases brings the need for special techniques to handle the student.  For example, if the student is quiet, passive, you'll need to draw him out.  It may take more than one conference to gain his trust and confidence in you as a reader.

Like the rest of the techniques for teaching writing, conferencing too takes practice to perfect.  It's worth it because students begin to see you in the role of coach and facilitator rather than evaluator.  They also come to recognize that writing is something that is nearly always in process and that readers comments and questions make a significant difference in the final product.  While conferencing is time consuming, its tremendous value cannot be overstated.   Frequent comments on my and my colleagues teaching evaluations refer to the conference: "conferencing really helped my writing," "those office meetings showed that the teacher really cared about me and my writing," etc.

## WHAT IS THE TEACHER'S ROLE IN A WRITING CONFERENCE?

As the teacher, you have a number of responsibilities toward conducting a successful writing conference. The list of six conferencing tips that follows is a synthesis of what Harris, in Teaching One-to-One: The Writing Conference, and Carnicelli, in "The Writing Conference: A One-to-One Conversation," outline.

1.  Use language carefully. Both verbal and nonverbal language affect the students' receptivity. Be certain to monitor the speed at which you speak, and use vocabulary that your students can understand. This can be tricky because this language feature varies with each student. For example, some students may be able to handle some of the composition jargon, while others cannot. The physical setting also gives your students clues about the conference. Set the student up so that she is sitting beside you, not across the desk from you.

2.  Listen carefully to what your student says. While this sounds like a simple statement, it is difficult to do. As teachers, it is our natural inclination to want to teach, and that means to speak. In this case, though, listening must take priority. Graves recommends waiting for fifteen seconds before responding (99). Try it--it seems like a long time. But students need time to formulate their answers and their thoughts, and to do that requires some silence. Harris says to listen for two kinds of information: the answers to your questions and to writers talking about their own writing (56). I might add a third: listen for writers' questions, which sometimes surface as comments or as concerns to which you can respond.

3.  Question your students, especially asking open-ended questions. Open-ended questions encourage a wide range of responses, ask for opinions, not just a yes or a no. Murray suggests that we ask questions like "What's the most important thing you have to say?" or "What questions will your reader ask you, and when?" (145). Moving students into larger considerations of audience, purpose, focus, and so on are essential. Focusing on these global concerns, rather than the local concerns of punctuation, for example, encourages the student to look at the whole piece of discourse and its effectiveness.

Asking the right questions can accomplish a lot in the writing conference. Harris suggests that questions "clarify for us and for students what problems the students are having, and they can move students away from minor editing by suggesting a more appropriate agenda of writing concerns. And they can also indicate that a real search or discovery is going on" (63).

For example, Graves (1983) recommends the following kinds of questions:

- Open the conference: How is it going? What are you writing about? Where are you now in your draft?

- Deal with the process: What do you think you'll do next? How will you develop/organize/revise? If you were to put new information there, how would you do it?

- Reveal the writer's development: How did you go about writing this? How did you go about choosing your subject? What do you think of this piece of writing?

- Deal with basic structures: What is this paper about? Is there anything else you might do with this piece?

- Cause a temporary loss of control, to challenge a confident student to think through a problem outside the conference: What does your ending have to do with your beginning? Are you ready to handle a problem like this? (107-17).

4.  Observe your students during their conferences to assess their problems and their progress (Harris, 65). To do this Harris recommends comparing conferences, the kinds of questions, comments, and concerns that the students have about their writing. Can they express themselves more clearly than before, articulate troublesome spots, strengths, and weaknesses in their writing? Are they more sensitive to their readers' needs?

This kind of observational data lets us know how the student is progressing over the course of several writing projects. About this, Harris says, "In this kind of observation we are placing students' present actions and words in a perspective that allows us to note their growth and progress over a semester or through a series of conferences" (65).

Harris also recommends using the conference as a place to diagnose the causes of students' writing problems. As she says, the conference allows you to look beyond the piece of writing to the writer herself. Thus, if a grammatical problem surfaces, the student may recognize it as a problem, but not really know the rule, but still be able to try to solve the problem.

Last, Harris recommends that we can assess whether students need new strategies to assist them with their writing (Harris, 65-66).

5.  Model ways of solving writing problems for the student. You can demonstrate, for example, how to brainstorm. Then, ask the student to practice the technique you have modeled. Watching you struggle with a particular writing technique will offer the student some encouragement to keep trying herself. All too often students believe that we write well with little effort. To see that it takes you some effort to perform is encouraging to a struggling writer.

6.  Tell students ways to solve problems, or explain alternate ways to develop their topics. Even though we like to encourage students to solve their own problems in writing, sometimes it is not feasible to do that. Discovering bibliographic conventions, for example, is less productive than your simply telling the students how, precisely, to do it. This, however, is a judgment call on your part--to know when it makes more sense to give the lesson than to allow students to discover the answer themselves.

## WHAT ARE CONFERENCING'S BENEFITS?

Conferencing has many benefits, but the following are probably its most salient (Harris, 1986; Carnicelli, 1980):

1.  The teacher's time is used more efficiently. Because the teacher is talking directly to the student, the teacher's responses are more effective simply because the teacher can say more in a shorter period of time than if she is writing comments in her

office. She also has the student handy to clarify the intentions in the paper. An added advantage is that the student most likely learns more from the personal, oral response than from written responses.

2.  Students are individualizing their own instruction. Since in class, writing instruction takes on a general approach, conferencing gives students the much needed and valuable instruction for their own individual writing needs. It is especially important keeping in mind that writing is an individual skill and students develop it at individual rates. For this reason, the conference is a good place for the teacher to individualize instruction too. The teacher can provide specific writing techniques and advice to a specific writer for a particular situation.

3.  Conferences promote independent or self learning. The focus is on the student's response, not on the teacher's presentation, not on the class's needs and responses. In this situation, the student is not put in a reactive position if the teacher allows the student to make the first response in the conference. In other words, the teacher should let the student comment about his own writing first (Carnicelli, 109).

The conference can be an important ingredient in teaching students to rewrite their papers. It should present opportunities for students to talk about their papers, to learn strategies specific to their own needs, and to experience encouragement in their own quests to become better writers.

In addition to the writing conference with the teacher, students can receive excellent feedback from one another if they are systematically taught strategies for responding to one another's writing.

## STUDENTS HELPING STUDENTS: THE WRITING RESPONSE GROUP

Peer response groups bring together the composing process and the interpersonal process. About this, Karen Spear (1988) says:

In writing classes, group interaction reinforces the notion that writing is not just what you end up with but the activities you undertake in creating it: the process as well as the product. Thus group interaction potentially helps to offset the artificiality of a writing class by enlarging the reading audience, introducing problems of genuine communication, supplying multiple perspectives and points of view, and modifying the teacher's many complex roles as instigator, helper, critic, audience, and evaluator (4).

If the teacher is the only one who reads students' work, the students get tangled in the web of writing what they thought the teacher wanted. They confuse what the teacher believed the students ought to say with what the students really did want to say. So, if students learn to assist in the revising process, they can both give and receive guidance from readers who talk about how it felt to read the piece. They can respond as a reader to the piece, making recommendations for adding details, illustrations, explanations, and examples, or they can recommend deleting excess information; they can recommend a new order to the piece. By doing this for one another, they come to share in "the communal enterprises of knowing and sharing what is known" (Spear, 6). Bruffee says that when students read one another's work, they "ask where their peers are coming from as the author of a given essay and where they hope to go with the piece. Thus, writing groups, whether formal or informal, help students learn how writers behave and to become helpful and productive members of the community of effective writers" (Bruffee, "Teaching," 28).

Students learn a lot by interacting with one another. Freshman composition is only the beginning of collaboration--the workplace may also demand much collaborative work, especially in writing tasks. Besides these far reaching effects, students in response groups are teaching one another. They exchange ideas about how to develop writing tasks, how to achieve their purposes in writing, how to address a given audience. Somewhat removed from the teacher, they can learn to provide positive and honest feedback for one another.

Students are not, for the most part, used to working in groups, especially to giving advice that can influence their peer's grade, so they do need practice. They need practice knowing what to look for and how to advise. They need practice not to respond like the teacher they might have once known who always corrected grammar. You can help ease them into peer response groups by structuring a sequence of activities to prepare the students and by giving them specific guidance in performing the tasks.

## STRUCTURING PEER RESPONSE GROUP ACTIVITIES

Like constructing writing assignments themselves, peer response activities need to be sequenced for the students to become comfortable and proficient at responding to one another's work. Beaven (1977) recommends that four stages be implemented in preparing students to be peer evaluators in writing response groups.

1.  Pair students up, preferably students who do not know each other. Give them a short task of about fifteen to twenty minutes to work on. This task can be a writing task or not. One of the activities that appear later in this chapter about revising for style would work here.

2.  A group of four students work on a similar short task of about fifteen to twenty minutes. Have the students change groups after a single task so they work in several groups on short tasks. This is a good place to have a group model the activity in front of the class, too.

3.  Assign students to work in a group of four on a longer project. You can assign students to groups based on one of several criteria: similar ability, diverse ability, similar or diverse personality characteristics, or student choice. You can, at this point, also evaluate the group process, its dynamics and interpersonal skills.

4.  Last, have students evaluate one another's work. In this stage, use the same criteria to place students in groups--your choice or theirs (148).

When you reach the last stage with your students, you will have other things to think about too: will you keep a writing group together for a long time or will you give students the opportunity to work with a variety of groups? There are benefits to either system. If students stay with the same group, they benefit from becoming familiar with one another and comfortable. If they change groups, they may benefit from the strengths of other students.

You also need to decide whether to give grade credit to students for responding to one another. By giving them a grade, you express the value of this in your overall plan for their growth in writing. Sometimes students need a grade to keep them motivated, though of course it is also possible to have their own improved writing be the motivating factor.

In addition to the four stages that Beaven recommends, I advise involving the whole class in a response session that models the kind of questions and response they will be giving to one another.  To do this, distribute a sample photocopied essay, preferably one that responds to a task similar to the one that the students will be writing.  Provide the students with the questions that they will answer about their own projects, and work as a group on responding to the essay.  This could also be done as Beaven's stage three project.

## THE PEER RESPONSE GROUP: WHAT TO DO

The purpose of having students work in a writing response group of their peers is to draw their attention to what they see as effective writing.  To revise their essays, students need readers who will listen to, look at, and respond to the piece of writing at hand.  The reader's job is to advise the writer if the writing is not clear enough.  This type of writing activity focuses on form and content, what the writer wants to say compared to what the writer did say.  As the teacher, your job is twofold: getting ready for the class and conducting the response group session.

## BEFORE RESPONSE GROUPS MEET

Before the class day on which you'll engage in peer review, prepare a checklist of procedures and task for the students.  These give the students confidence that they are doing it "right."  In these checklists, discourage looking for errors such as grammar, spelling, punctuation.  Lindemann recommends generating these lists together with the students before the day that they'll use them.  This gives you a chance to involve the students in setting the standards and defining what constitutes good writing (187).  As Lindemann goes on to say, the hidden agenda is to get students to develop the criteria that we would use in evaluating their work.

There are a number of ways to present these checklists to students.  One is to provide an extensive list like the one that Lindemann (187-88) asked her students to generate.  This particular adaptation from Lindemann is designed to be used by the writer herself as a checklist of things to do; however, it could easily be tailored for a reader's response, too.

## Subject, Audience, Purpose

1.  What is the critical issue I want to address about this subject?

2.  Who will be my audience? What do they want to know about the subject? What do they now know about it?

3.  Is the subject important enough to write about? Will the reader believe the paper is worthwhile?

4.  What verb most clearly expresses the purpose of the paper: (tells a story, compares two things, describes something)?

5.  Decide whether the first paragraph addresses my first four priorities as listed above. Revise as needed if it does not.

## Organization

6.  How many points of support should I use? Are there any points for supporting the main idea need to be added, deleted, elaborated?

7.  How many paragraphs do I need to discuss each point?

8.  Is this the best order of points and paragraphs? Most effective? Are changes in order needed?

9.  How do paragraphs and sentences move from one point to another? Consider whether readers need more or fewer forecasting statements or transitions to make necessary connections.

## Paragraphing (Consider these issues for each paragraph)

10. What is the role of each paragraph? How does it relate to the one that precedes and follows?

11. Identify the topic idea.  Will readers locate it easily?

12. What sentences were used to develop the topic idea?  Is it the right number?  Could there be better examples, reasons, or details?

13. How well do the paragraphs flow?  Decide how its levels of generality should be built, how much sentence variety is needed, and whether to add better transitions.

## Sentences (Consider these issues for each sentence)

14. What sentences in the paper look good to me?  What ones look bad?  Try to determine why.

15. Do I "show" what my sentences say? Look for chances to replace vague nouns, verbs, adjectives, and adverbs (people, things, this/that, aspect, etc.) with more specific ones.

16. Have I cut wordiness at all levels? (Apply the "paramedic method")[1]

17. Could I combine some sentences together?  Will this be more concise or more effective?

18. Can I add more vivid adjectives or adverbs or more lively verbs?

## Last Check

19. Are spelling and punctuation accurate?  Focus on the kinds of previous I have made.

20. Do I like the way the paper ends?  Did I deliver on the "promises" made at the beginning?

21. Have I missed important parts of the assignment?

22. What are the strongest features of this paper?  Why?  What kinds of features will need work in the next paper?

Another possibility with response group checklists is to provide only a few, but very broadly inclusive questions.  Beaven recommends the following questions:

1. Identify the best section of the composition and describe what makes it effective.

2. Identify a sentence, a group of sentences, or a paragraph that needs revision, and revise it as a group, writing the final version on the back of the paper.

3. Identify one (or two) things the writer can do to improve his or her next piece of writing.  Write these goals on the first page at the top.

4. (After the first evaluation, the following question should come first.)  What were the goals the writer was working on?  Were they reached?  If not, identify those passages that need improvement and as a group revise those sections, writing final versions on the back of the paper.  If revisions are necessary, set up the same goals for the next paper and delete question 3 (149).

A third possibility is to key your response group checklists to the writing assignment itself.  In developing peer response guides for the sample assignment from Chapter 1 of this book, you might end up with the following kinds of specific and general questions.

1. What did you like best about this essay?  Why?

2. Does the writer make the significance of this event/person clear?  If yes, summarize in your own words that significance-- what did the author learn?  If no, suggest how this significance can be communicated clearly.

3. Comment on the organization of this paper. If it is well organized, state what you liked about it. If it is not well organized, state how the writer can improve the organization.

4. After reading this essay, is there anything MORE that you would like to know?

5. The beginning of an essay has to interest the reader immediately if it is going to succeed. Read the first sentence of the paper and rate its "appeal factor" on a scale of 1 to 10. Give advice on how to make this sentence a 10.

6. Do exactly the same thing you just did for the whole first paragraph. Suggest how the writer can make it clearer, better, or more interesting.

7. After reading this essay, was there anything that you thought was unnecessary? Tell the writer what s/he might take out for the final draft.

8. Comment on the conclusion of the essay. If you think it is effective, tell the writer what you liked. If it could be more effective, help the writer revise it.

9. On the draft, find a "telling" sentence. Ask the writer to write a showing paragraph for that sentence.

10. What one recommendation would you make for this writer to improve this essay?

These ten questions are keyed to the writing assignment and to the kinds of activities that we have been doing in class (e. g., "showing writing"). Often, I divide these ten questions into two sets; each reviewer prepares two different sets of responses. If I do this, I group the questions so that the person making the responses is working in on single large rhetorical category, such as content.

Once you have prepared the checklists for the students to use in class, you are ready. Students, however, need also to be prepared for class. Ask them to bring multiple copies of their work in progress. These can be computer printouts, photocopies, or dittoes. This way, each respondent can have a draft to work on, and to write comments directly on.

If you are placing the students in groups, determine such placement before class time.

## RESPONSE GROUPS IN SESSION

Once you and the students get to class, you'll need to quickly organize the groups and get to work.

1. Form the response groups. Either you have chosen the group members or you will allow the students to choose their own groups.

2. Distribute the handout with the directions for how to proceed and the checklist of comments to make.

3. Have students distribute the copies of their drafts to the members of their response groups.

4. I ask students to take turns in their response groups and READ ALOUD their drafts. Often a student will inject a piece with meaning orally that he or she has not done in writing. This helps the responders to know what the writer meant to say.

5. After everyone has read his or her essay, and received oral feedback, set them to work on the written comments and discussion of each essay in turn. You might consider having them take these home to complete. Sometimes the privacy of working on reading, thinking, and commenting helps a lot. If you do this, allow time the next class period for the groups to reconvene and talk about the comments.

6. Move around the groups as they work. Settle confusion about the task, pose questions to writers and readers, and keep people on task, but try not to give advice about writer's work.

One small word of caution: Don't be discouraged by some groups working well while others do not. Like the classroom, group dynamics vary tremendously from one group to another, even from one day to another. Some groups click immediately, some need prodding, some don't work very well.

Working in writing response groups has benefits for teacher and students alike. Largely, the benefits accrue as the students become more adept at recognizing effective writing and being able to identify strong and weak areas of both their own writing and that of the other writers.

WORKS CITED Chapter 8

Beaven, Mary H.  "Individualized Goal Setting, Self-evaluation, and Peer Evaluation."  Evaluating Writing: Describing, Measuring, Judging.  Eds. Charles R. Cooper and Lee Odell.  Urbana, Illinois: National Council of Teachers of English, 1977.  135-156.

Bruffee, Kenneth.  "Teaching Writing Through Collaboration."  Learning in Groups.  Eds. Clark Bouton and Russell Y. Garth.  San Francisco: Jossey-Bass, 1983.

---.  "Collaborative Learning and 'The Conversation of Mankind.'"  College English 46 (1984): 635-652.

Carnicelli, Thomas A.  "The Writing Conference: A One-to-One Conversation."  Eight Approaches to Teaching Composition.  Eds. Timothy R. Donovan and Ben W. McClelland.  Urbana, Illinois: National Council of Teachers of English, 1980.  101-132.

Emig, Janet.  "We Are Trying Conferences."  English Journal, 49 (1960): 223-228.

Garrison, Roger.  "One-to-One: Tutorial Instruction in Freshman Composition."  New Directions for Community Colleges 2 (1974): 55-84.

---.  How a Writer Works.  Rev ed.  New York: Harper and Row, Publishers, 1985.

Graves, Donald.  Writing: Teachers and Children at Work.  Portsmouth, NH: Heinemann, 1983.

Harris, Muriel.  Teaching One-to-One: The Writing Conference.  Urbana, Illinois: National Council of Teachers of English, 1986.

Lindemann, Erika.  A Rhetoric for Writing Teachers.  2nd ed.  New York: Oxford University Press, 1987.

Murray, Donald.   "The Listening Eye: Reflections on the Writing Conference." College English 41 (1979): 13-18.

---.   "Teaching the Other Self." College Composition and Communication 33 (1982): 140-147.

Spear, Karen.   Sharing Writing: Peer Response Groups in English Classes. Portsmouth, NH: Boynton/Cook Publishers, 1988.

## END NOTE

[1]   The paramedic method is one designed by Richard Lanham and adapted by Lindemann in A Rhetoric for Writing Teachers on page 182. To apply this method, the writer circles prepositions, circles forms of "is," etc. looking for ways to reduce what Lanham calls the "lard" factor--too many unnecessary words.

# CHAPTER 9:
# REWRITING--EDITING AND
# PROOFREADING

Editing and proofreading are generally narrowly defined terms. Thus, says Graser, "For many student writers, not being able to distinguish what they have written from what they mean makes proofreading [and editing] more necessary and infinitely more difficult" (110). In the grand scheme of producing a written product, your students should edit their papers primarily as a final stage--having developed and revised their prose rigorously beforehand. Editing fine tunes the "surface" level of their work. In one last careful consideration of what he or she wants to say, the student thinks one more time about how the audience will receive the message and how the purpose will be achieved. To be certain that deviations from the standard written language don't distract the reader, the student looks both for "surface" errors and for syntactical and stylistic rough spots. Specifically, during this final polish of the piece, your students

- touch up paragraph and sentence connections,

- refine specific word choices,

- correct any mechanical errors in spelling, punctuation, capitalization, and so on so that these don't deviate from convention and distract the readers, and

- fine tune the style.

This chapter talks about some of the possible sources of errors that occur in students' writing and surveys the things that your students should work on during the editing stage of their writing.

## THE ORIGIN OF SOME ERRORS

If we are going to attempt to reduce some of our students' errors in writing, we need to think about why they are making those errors. Shaughnessy says that "they [composition students] are beginners and must, like all beginners, learn by making mistakes" (5). This may be true, but like a golf coach, we must understand the sources of the students' errors and difficulties, and coach them into a standard use of the language when they write.  We can help students by being sensitive to the possible sources of some of their deficiencies in writing.  Four important factors--spoken language, second-language interference, dialect patterns, and partially-remembered rules--contribute largely to students' surface-level errors in writing (Glaser, 106-110).

Students' spoken language can be a source for errors in written language, whether English is their primary language or not.  For one thing, students often write as they speak.  For example, if words sound alike (i.e., homonyms), students are likely to spell them the same (e.g., here and hear; there, their, and they're).  They also tend to punctuate as if they were talking, which can result in a paper peppered by commas or periods inappropriately placed.  Glaser says that "Relating reading, writing, and speaking means that students can learn that not all pauses equal periods, not all pauses equal a mark at all, not all published punctuation is exactly alike, but that no published punctuation misleads the reader" (116).

Unfortunately, some students have been advised to punctuate by considering pauses in spoken English.  These students who have been told that pauses in their speech equate to punctuation can be helped in two ways:

1.  Tell them that at one time, people actually believed that that was a helpful way to teach students about punctuation, but that it has since proven to cause problems for students.  This kind of explanation does not insult them or a favorite high school English teacher who used this strategy.

2.  Using a good handbook, their own writing, or another resource, teach the students that there are a specific number of concrete rules for using each piece of punctuation.  For example, there are five specific uses for the semicolon.

In "How 'Normal' Speaking Leads to 'Erroneous' Punctuating," Danielewicz and Chafe maintain that inexperienced writers do not necessarily lack the knowledge to place punctuation properly, but that they do not really know what commas and periods are for, and that "their 'errors' come from assuming that the uses of spoken language can be transferred to writing without change" (213).  Danielewicz and Chafe conclude their study by saying:

What are the implications for the teaching of writing?  We believe that it is salutary for teachers to be aware that inexperienced writers may actually be doing a good job of representing in writing the already extensive knowledge they have of speaking.  If their nonstandard punctuations can be seen as inappropriate extensions of spoken language into a different medium, not as random errors, then teachers can concentrate on pointing out specific ways in which the requirements of writing differ from those of speaking (225).

Sometimes you will have students who are not native speakers of English.  This second language interference can cause some problems.  Knowing a bit about the structure of some major language types can help.  Languages vary a great deal in some of the following ways: placement of the adjective before or after the noun it describes, time markers in verbs (some languages actually do not mark time in their verbs), and gender assignment--unlike English some languages assign a gender to all nouns.  Simply being aware of the fact that languages vary tremendously in syntactic structure and then identifying those students who have foreign-language interference can help your teaching.  Often your college will have expert help available for these students at a writing center or through a linguistics department.

Dialect patterns may also play an important role in students' error patterns.  The language that they hear most frequently is most likely the one that will account for linguistic difficulties in their written work.  Thus, dialects that treat verbs differently, for example, will cause some interference in the student's written work.

To address this issue with your students--which may be a sensitive one for your students--explain a bit about regional dialects in the country so that the students don't think that they are alone in being different.  Explain that even within a relatively small geographic area these differences occur.  Then, emphasize the need to communicate in writing in a way that all people who speak the language can understand.  That is the rationale for learning the standard written English that you are teaching.

Many students also come to us with many partially-remembered rules which interfere with their production of standard written English.  Students try to do what they've been told to do, but with so many rules in English grammar, they often remember those rules only in part.  For example, somewhere they remember that there are a multitude of rules for using commas, for instance, so they attempt to remember these rules as they write.  The result is often a paper that is peppered with punctuation, and often that punctuation is inaccurate, causing some real problems in conveying the meaning that they intend to convey.

Working out individual student's problems using the rules of grammar provides an opportunity to use a handbook as a tool for individualizing instruction. Both as an offshoot of your conferencing with students and as a result of your review of their group work, you can make specific assignments for students who have specific needs. The "error log" that is described later in this chapter works very well with individual students.

## TEACHING EDITING AND PROOFREADING

Teaching students about editing and proofreading can be a difficult task. We teachers often have our own sets of idiosyncratic ideas when it comes to correctness. Some of us get overly enthusiastic about a single grammatical rule, such as "the comma always comes inside the quotation marks." In this zeal we give too much importance to a single principle, sometimes one that does not even cause readers to misread the text. How do we avoid imposing our idiosyncrasies too enthusiastically on our students? Once again, think about the purpose for writing and the readers' needs--mechanical errors that distract readers from the intended meaning need attention.

This sounds simple, until you realize that seldom do all of your students have the same needs when it comes to teaching the editing phase of writing. What do you do? Generally speaking, if the class shows signs of having similar problems, you can teach the whole class one of these editing principles. It is more than likely that the whole class will need to know about some issues such as developing style, for example, but only some of them will need to work on comma rules.

In the case of the few who need specific instruction on one principle, teach them in small groups of students who have similar needs. You can do this as part of your class activities or you can send students to your campus's writing center. If you do integrate editing workshops into your classroom instruction, devote a class period to workshopping these skills. Spend a few minutes with each of several small groups while the other students are working on their writing. As Graser says, "If teachers can begin to identify the similarities underlying many apparently different sentence errors and can help students see their own patterns of error, teachers and students can work together toward producing sentences that are long, complex, and syntactically sound" (115).

When you teach students to recognize and correct these kinds of editing and proofreading errors, keep the following tips in mind:

1.  Focus on <u>one principle</u> at a time. Addressing more than one major type of error often is overwhelming to students, no matter how small it seems to you. So, if using commas and not periods with introductory adverbial clauses is a problem for one small group of students, concentrate your teaching efforts on just that. This works well if you also have them construct a checklist to which they can add items over the course of the semester. At the end of the semester, you'll both be surprised at what they have mastered.

2.  Use <u>sentence combining</u> so that students will learn to manipulate a wide variety of sentence patterns. While sentence combining is not a panacea, it gives students a way to work with punctuation and the nuances of the language. They are surprised to learn that a number of sentences can be combined in a variety of ways, and that each of those ways creates a slightly different meaning. These kinds of exercises can come from their own work or from one of the good references that is available (c. f., Strong).

    In recommending sentence combining exercises, Graser says that students can learn to "use complex patterns they unconsciously were familiar with . . . [S]tudents learn to control and punctuate more complex syntactic structures and even to use them in their own writing" (116).

3.  Teach students to help themselves and one another to locate common errors. The students can rely on their response groups to help them find errors. In fact, having specialists in the group is one possibility: one person is a fragment specialist, while another is a comma specialist, and so on.

4.  Often having students read their essays backwards from finish to start will isolate any remaining errors.

## INTERVENTION EXERCISES

Aside from these general tips on teaching editing and proofreading, you can introduce a specific lesson just before an essay is due. Timed at just the right moment, these exercises enter into the final stages of the composing of an essay and make the students sensitive to particular issues of paragraph structure, the words they've chosen, their use of mechanics (e.g., punctuation, capitalization, spelling), and the style of their essays. The following sections of this chapter talk about specific intervention exercises that are designed to target individual issues in writing:

- Overall paragraph structure
- Lexical cues and cohesion in paragraph structure
- Sentences
- Word choice
- Mechanics and
- Style.

## OVERALL PARAGRAPH STRUCTURE

When students have what is essentially a finished draft for an assignment, ask them to reconsider the superstructure of their individual paragraphs, especially remembering the approaches to paragraphing that you taught. If you taught them Kerrigan and Metcalf paragraphs (discussed in an earlier chapter of this book), they may be able to dissect their own or one another's paragraphs for the structure that they recommend. Specifically, the following four activities provide useful practice in paragraphing for your students.

1. Locate a sample paragraph, either a student's or a published paragraph, but one that has a fairly good organizatinoal pattern as it stands. Place each sentence from the paragraph on a 3 X 5 card. With students in work groups of about four, have them decide how to order the sentences. Have them report to the class, and describe why they ordered the sentences the way that they did. Last, show them the original and discuss which order is the most appropriate and why.

2. Have students look at a sample paragraph and discuss how they might revise it to improve upon it. Have them recall the lessons you have given them on moving from the general to the specific, repeating key words to keep the same idea moving through the paragraph.

3. If this is not the students' first essay, have them revive and revise a paragraph from a former essay. Once the students have

revised an old paragraph, have them talk about what they did to revise it and why they did what they did. For example, did they change the order of sentences? Did they change individual words? Did they add or delete information from the paragraph? And so on.

4. Have small groups select a sentence from their rough drafts and ask the students in the group to write a "showing paragraph" based on that sentence.

## LEXICAL CUES AND COHESION IN PARAGRAPH STRUCTURES

An offshoot of the tagmemic strategy used for inventing material (discussed in an earlier chapter of this book), the six strategies that are discussed next provide lexical cues for constructing tight, cohesive paragraphs. These six intellectual strategies were developed by Lee Odell (1977) to diagnose writing problems and to measure growth in writing. However, these six strategies can also be used to show students some specific linguistic and grammatical cues that they can use to manipulate paragraph structure in very particular ways: to achieve a particular focus, to write contrast or classification, to present change, to show physical context, and to demonstrate sequence.[1]

### FOCUS

Looking at the grammatical subjects of their sentences can give students a real feel for their internal camera. Odell says, "This process of shifting focus and selecting detail is reflected not only in photography but in the syntax of our written and spoken language. If we examine grammatical focus--that is, the grammatical subject of each clause in a piece of discourse--we can learn a good bit about the way the talker or writer is perceiving and thinking" (109).

Odell recommends that we provide them with a passage such as the following from Mark Twain's Life on the Mississippi:

. . . the furnace doors are open and the fires glazing bravely; the upper decks are black with passengers; the captain stands by the big bell, calm, imposing, the envy of all; great volumes of the blackest smoke are rolling and tumbling out of the chimneys--a husbanded grandeur created with a bit of pitch-pine just before arriving at a town. . . . (109)

If students extract the subjects, they get a feel for how Twain was directing our attention from the furnace doors, to the upper decks, to the captain, to the volumes of black smoke. Having talked about the effectiveness of this strategy, have students do two exercises: imitate the paragraph of Twain's; extract the subjects from a paragraph of their own. This second activity is often useful because students often find that they have many subjects that are the same or that are lifeless, such as "it."

This passage from Dylan Thomas's "Quite Early One Morning" is an excellent one to use as a model for imitating. The students can imagine that they are sitting high above the campus, looking down on it as they imitate this passage.

The sun lit the sea-town, not as a whole . . . but in separate bright pieces. There, the quay shouldering out, nobody on it now but the gulls and the capstans like small men in tubular trousers. Here, the roof of the roof of the police station, black as a helmet, dry as a summons, sober as Sunday. There, the splashed church, with a cloud in the shape of a bell poised above it, ready to drift and ring. Here the chimneys of the pink-washed pub, the pub that was waiting for Saturday night as an over jolly girl waits for sailors.

The alternating "there" and "here" make for excellent opportunities to practice focusing.

## CONTRAST

To understand what something is, Odell says, we must also know what it is not. "Contrast," he says, "is operating when we make distinctions, when we have a sense of incongruity, or when we are aware of some disparity" (111). Thus, often our students can make themselves and their writing clear by answering the question, "What is this [the subject of the paper] NOT like?" In getting the answer to this question down on paper, it helps them to have practiced a bit with the linguistic cues the demonstrate a contrast exists in the paragraph or in the entire essay.

Odell presents the following example from Robert Coles' book, The South Goes North, to demonstrate contrast:

> My old man, he was no good.  He drank all the time. You can have it; I like beer, but I don't drink the way he did. They found him dead in some alley.  He was frozen to death, buried in snow.  Can you beat that!  And when they told her, my old lady, she didn't say anything.  She didn't cry.  She said she didn't even care.  She told me my father really had been dead for five years, and the Lord was just too busy to notice and call for him.  I thought she was fooling me, but she wasn't.  My old lady, anything she says she means (112).

Students examine this passage for the connectors, the comparative and superlative forms, the negative words including ones with negative affixes, and words that are synonymous with contrast, distinction, difference, and so on.  Connectors that show contrast include the following: or, nor, otherwise, but, however, nevertheless, on the other hand.  By comparative and superlative forms, Odell means words such as more/most, less/least, and forms that end in -er/-est. Negative words include no, not, without, nothing, and none, while the negative affixes include anti-, im-, in-, non-, -less, and so on.

Considering these linguistic cues, and others that demonstrate contrast, have students look at the Coles' paragraph to locate his instances of using contrast to make his point.  Have them look at their own writing in the same manner, or have them imitate the Coles paragraph.

## CLASSIFICATION

Much the same as pointing specifically to contrast, the use of classification in students' essays can help them look for ways that their subject is like other things or see what groups or categories of things they are working with.  To assist the students, have them look for instances in their writing where it would be helpful to answer the question, "What is this like?" (this being the subject that the students are writing about or the specific thing they are dealing with in a particular paragraph).

Linguistic cues for classification include sentence syntax: when a linking verb joins a subject with a predicate nominative, one of the noun phrases (the subject or the predicate) suggests a class while the other names the member.  For example, "The swimmer was a gold-medalist."  This sentence puts the subject, "swimmer" into the class of "gold-medal winners."

Other linguistic cues of classification include the use of phrases like "for example," "for instance," and so on.  Last, words that are synonymous with similar, resemble, and class are cues to the classification strategy, as are words that indicate metaphor (like, as, etc).

Odell uses the following example from R. M. Lumiansky's translation of Chaucer's "The Miller's Tale" to demonstrate how a writer uses classification to make his point clear:

> The young wife was pretty, with a body as neat and graceful as a weasel.  She wore a checked silk belt, and around her loins a flounced apron as white as fresh milk . . . her singing as loud and lively as a swallow's sitting on a barn.  In addition, she could skip about and play like any kid or calf following its mother . . . . She was a primrose, a trillium, fit to grace the bed of any lord or to marry any good yeoman (113-114).

Again students can look to this passage for ways that they author labels "the young wife" in this tale.  Having located the cues, students can look to their own writing for places where this can be modeled.

### CHANGE

Often change is part of the subject that students write about-- the nature and extent of its change over time and circumstances.  To both teach and recognize how change operates in written discourse, Odell recommends that we look for the following linguistic cues: "verb, noun, adjective, or adverb forms of the word 'change' or a synonym for 'change'."  He also includes as linguistic cues verb phrases which include "began" or "stop" plus a verbal or a phrase that can be written to include "become" (118).

### PHYSICAL CONTEXT

Like change, references to the context in which the students' subjects occur make their writing better.  Thus, Odell recommends that studer: he encouraged to use frequent, where appropriate, references to the actual physical context. The linguistic cues that show physical context include the following: "nouns that refer to a geographical location (e.g., the name of a city, a geographic region, a point on a map), an object in a physical setting (e.g., a house or tree), a sensory property of a physical setting (e.g., the sound of wind in the trees)" (119).

SEQUENCE

Students' subjects frequently are important if placed in a particular sequence of events, their own lives, other people's actions, social occurrences, and so on. Thus, working with them on developing clear sequence in their writing is important. Odell identifies the following as linguistic cues to sequence: time sequence is marked by adverbial elements that indicate "that something existed before, during, or after a moment in time. For example, then, when, next, later, meanwhile, subsequently, previously, at that moment, all indicate a sequence of events over time. Logical sequence is marked by "words implying a cause-effect relationship. For example: because, therefore, since, consequently, and the phrase if . . . then" (120).

Many of the ideas that Odell presents in these six intellectual strategies for use in writing we commonly think of as transitional devices. But this framework makes them especially concrete and identifiable. In talking about a specific piece of writing, Odell makes a comment that reflects what we often find ourselves thinking about a particular piece of writing:

> The organization is clear. And there are no errors in punctuation or spelling. But the paper is terribly dull. It gives no sense of the complexity, the drama, the interest of its subject. It reflects no real insight into the topic (127).

By having students examine their writing very carefully at the editing stage of their writing can result in papers that are not only correct, but also creative and analytical. As Odell says, "We'll have to teach her how" (127).

## SENTENCE-LEVEL EDITING

Carefully constructed and fine tuned sentences are another hallmark of the editing stage of writing. Two particular kinds of exercises help students to view sentence-level editing as an important part of finishing their essays: sentence combining and generating (or cumulative) sentences.

Sentence combining exercises are essentially exercises in embedding descriptive material, coordinate, or subordinate clauses into an existing main clause. Winterowd (1975), writing about the work of Mellon, who introduced the idea of sentence combining, says that this approach to grammar is "nothing more that an attempt to give an account of what every speaker of a language knows intuitively. . . . In other words, the language affords us the means to embed sentence within sentence within sentence. . . . And it goes without saying that embedding devices (in the jargon, transformations) are the single most powerful instrument that the language affords us" (365-6).

Embedding polishes a writer's prose by turning sequences of short simple sentences into a single more syntactically mature sentence. Having the knowledge to choose between a series of short, choppy sentences and one long fluid sentence is important in the context of audience and purpose: sometimes short, choppy sentences will be preferable, and others, the longer sentence will work better. Sentence combining activities help students to appreciate some of their editing options.

While sentence combining shows students ways to produce a variety of sentences that are different syntactically, work with generative (or cumulative) sentences looks at the sentence in terms of layers of meaning. Christensen says that "The foundation, then, for a generative or productive rhetoric of the sentence is that composition is essentially a process of addition" (130). He maintains that every sentence has as its core a main clause stated in general or abstract terms. "With the main clause stated, the forward movement of the sentence stops, the writer shifts down to a lower level of generality or abstraction or to singular terms, and goes back over the same ground at this lower level" (131-2). This means that as a student writes a sentence, he continues to make his point by adding or generating ideas that elaborate upon the main clause. Each of these elaborations is at a more specific level of generality or abstraction. By teaching students the process of cumulative sentence building, we teach them a skill that "serves the needs of both the writer and the reader, the writer by compelling him to examine his thought, the reader by letting him into the writer's thought" (131).

The essential difference between these two sentence construction techniques is that sentence combining is viewed as one that embeds ideas while generative sentences are viewed as sentences that accumulate ideas.

## SENTENCE COMBINING EXERCISES

Sentence combining is not only fun, but it is also instructive in a number of ways for students in their roles as editors. Introducing sentence combining as an intervention activity shows students that skilled writing is a craft that only takes practice, that it can be learned. By working with sentence combining exercises, students can become more skilled at some of the advanced ways of constructing sentences and paragraphs from their ideas. In doing this, students see nuances of meaning by shifting words, phrases, and clauses around. They come to appreciate the varieties in both meaning and style that changing the word order can make. They also experiment with punctuation as they complete sentence combining exercises. Cooper states: "In other words, the teacher can accelerate growth toward written syntactic maturity if he can help students increase the amount of modification around their nouns and help them use noun substitutes (phrases and clauses) in place of single-word nouns" (119). The same is true for verbs.

Sentence combining works very well with students' own work, if they have a previous paper or spots in the draft in progress that they need to edit by combining sentences. Once they have been introduced to sentence combining, a simple "combine some of these" written in the margin, says a lot to them about the kinds of editing they might want to consider. Before students can do this, however, they probably need some practice with published exercises, of which there are many. There may be some in your handbook or textbook; or you might create a batch of your own.

Strong, in Sentence Combining: A Composing Book, recommends moving students from easy exercises to more difficult and longer lists of combinations, searching for "multiple answers (or options) rather that for a single 'right' answer" (x). To do this, complete a sample exercise as a whole class to demonstrate all the possibilities that exist with one small set of sentences. For example:

The students are in college.
The students are freshmen.
They are in class.

They are writing.
They are writing essays.

These five sentences can combine in several ways one of which is the following: The college freshmen students are in class writing essays. From one simple example such as this one, you can demonstrate the differences in style among saying "college freshmen students," "freshmen college students," "students who are freshmen in college," and so on. The five sentences could also be combined to produce a compound sentence: The college freshmen are in class, and they are writing. The combinations are really endless with even a simple example such as this one. Through exercises like sentence combining you want your students to recognize that writing well is a craft that involves making choices, and that as editors, they can have much control over it.

Combining sentences can involve simply piling up the adjectives; it can involve adding, deleting, and substituting elaborate phrases. The more skilled your students get at recognizing sentence patterns, the more they will perform elaborate combinations of sentences. Strong recommends teaching sentence combining exercises in the following order:

Phase 1: Combine sentence groups in as many ways as possible. Have students record the varieties, and compare them with one another. You consider giving a reward to the student who can produce the most sentences from a group of sentences.

Phase 2: Once students have the hang of combining sentences freely (Phase 1), have them work with model sentences and imitating the models. This requires more work on your part if you are going to construct your own exercises. You'll need to have a model sentence (a sentence that is composed of several levels of meaning) that you want your students imitate. Then, you'll need to construct a set of simple sentences that will combine to produce a sentence pattern like the model. Once the students have worked through the exercise, you'll ask the students to write a sentence of their own using this pattern. The following example is from Strong's book:

The simple sentences . . .
"Harold shuffled to the front of the room.
Harold knotted his shoulders.

Harold jammed his hands into his pockets" (157).

The two-level sentence pattern . . .
"Harold shuffled to the front of the room, knotting his shoulders and jamming his hands into his pockets" (157).

The exercise . . .
"The present moment is electric.
The present moment sparks with life.
The present moment crackles with possibilities.
The possibilities are untried" (164).

Next, students combine the exercise sentences to make a sentence that has the same pattern as the two-level sentence in the example. This group would combine to form the sentence, "The present moment is electric, sparkling with life and crackling with untried possibilities."

Last, have students locate a spot in their own work where they can construct a sentence with the same pattern.

It's good to remember that students may produce awkward combinations at first. Strong says, "At first a good number of your students will probably produce elaborate and disastrously convoluted sentences. Do not panic . . . . The process of elaboration and sentence expansion is, of course, a first step in the generative process; the next step is tightening and compressing, making the prose more lithe and muscled" (xvii).


## GENERATING SENTENCES

Elaborating sentences by filling them up with detail is another way to get students to look at editing sentences. Christensen (1963; 1967) introduced the notion of the generative sentence, claiming that all sentences originate as simple sentences consisting of a subject and a verb; he calls these "kernel sentences." He maintains that beyond that core, we add clauses, adjectives, phrases, adverbs, and so on. As in "showing writing," if we have our students practice generating sentences that are loaded with modification, they see once again how good sentences are built by their writers.

Introduce this editing activity of generating sentences by putting a kernel sentence on the board. For example, one of the following works well:

The custodian fell.
The dog barked.
The audience applauded.
The rose bloomed.

Next, have students brainstorm elaboration for both the subject and the verb. Often, you'll end up with a silly sentence that is overloaded with modification, but this too helps to make your point about editing sentences. Once you have completed exercises with the students generating sentences, put them to work on their own or on their classmates' papers looking for sentences to elaborate.


## CORRECTING SENTENCES: THE "ERROR LOG"

The "error log," developed by Tommy Boley, is one of the most effective means of having students address their essay's surface features. To implement the error log, Boley recommends doing the following: When you grade student papers, place a check mark (✓) in the margin beside a line that contains an error. The student's job is to use the handbook or other rresources to locate the type of error, identify it, explain what they did, and correct it. Keeping a running account of these errors in a spiral notebook helps some students.

Graded credit can be given in a variety of ways and can be incremented over the course of the semester. Thus, for example, with students' first essays, I do a couple of things to motivate them: I underline the location of the error as best I can; I devote a full class to an "error log" workshop; and creditwise, I subtract ½ of a point from their actual essay grade. For each error that they correct, I add a full point on to the grade. Beginning with the second essay, I subtract a full point and give them equal credit for the error log work they do.

Students get the following instructions for completing an error log entry (Boley):

1. Name the type of error. Identify where in your handbook you found it.
2. Write a sentence that analyzes what you need to do to correct the error.
3. Rewrite the sentence from your essay in which the error appears correcting the error.

Sample entry:

1.  Comma error. Section __ in the handbook.
2.  I have separated the subject and the verb by a comma.
3.  Our assignment for this week is to complete the final draft of the persuasive essay.


## WORD-LEVEL EDITING

Even at the word level, there are important lessons for our students to practice. For example, the difference between saying "holy matrimony," "wedlock," "marriage," "tied the knot," and "hitched" in the context of an essay is significant, and these seemingly ordinary word choices are often the most important. To help students to intervene at the word level, you can construct some word-level exercises fairly quickly. For instance, you can talk about levels of usage--the differences between formal, informal, and general language--by having students think about how they would relay the specifics of an experience to their parents, their closest friend, and an unrelated authority figure, such as the high school principal. You can also provide them with lists of words in a "neutral" category and have them brainstorm synonyms that are formal and informal. Along the same lines, you can also have them rewrite entire sentences from one level of usage or another.

Students often may need practice in distinguishing between "general" and "specific" words, "abstract" and "concrete" ones, and the difference between "denotative" and "connotative" meaning. To distinguish among levels of generality, you might have them begin with a large category, like "human being" and have them work on making this more specific until they can see how the more specific they are, the clearer the picture that the reader gets of the person or event or idea about which they are writing.

Distinguishing between "abstract" and "concrete" should be easy: if you can touch it or hold it and see it, it is concrete. Ideas, on the other hand, are abstract.

Similarly, the differences between "denotative" and "connotative" meanings become clear to students quickly. Point them in the direction of a dictionary for denotative meanings, and then ask them what kind of feelings the word conjures up. The second is connotative meaning. For example, the word "ghetto" really denotes a particular section of a city where a specific ethnic, racial, or national group lives. However, when we hear the word "ghetto," it connotes any number of attitudes and qualities about the people and the living conditions of the area designated as a ghetto.

Last, have your students understand the need to tighten up their prose by eliminating "deadwood"--those words that are unessential and accomplish nothing but add words to the piece. You can find long lists of these phrases in almost any composition book. For example,

| Shorten this . . . | To . . . |
|---|---|
| Due to the fact that | Because |
| At this point in time | Now |
| Circular in shape | Circular (or round) |

Often, passive verbs will create sentences that are longer than they need to be, and at the same time passive verbs often lead to writing that is less than clear. Beginning sentences with "there are" or "it is" can also lead to extra words and ambiguity. These kinds of grammatical features may be discussed in the textbook you are using; they will certainly appear in the handbook.

Besides lists of words and exercise sheets, there are a number of ways to get students to appreciate the differences that one word can make. Have them gather set of advertisements and look at the differences in word choice between two brands of automobile, for example. Sometimes a single product is advertised differently based on the magazine in which it is published--if a particular brand of cereal, for example, is advertised in a children's publication, the word choice is bound to be different from those used in an adult's publication.

When it comes to needing examples for editing practice, you and your students will be able to find endless sources for comparing word choices once you get going--newspapers, billboards, church bulletins, published literature both fiction and nonfiction, to name a few sources.

EDITING FOR STYLE

How to define and describe "style" may be one of the most difficult concepts you have to tackle. Little makes the concept of "style" clearer to a student than Walker Gibson's (1966) scheme of "tough, sweet, and stuffy." For that reason, I introduce it here in some detail as a means to demonstrate how an author may edit to achieve a particular style or voice in his writing.

Gibson claims that prose styles fall into one of three categories--Tough Talk, Sweet Talk, or Stuffy Talk. Tough Talk is that of a "hard man who has been around" while Sweet Talk refers "primarily to the blandishments of advertising," and Stuffy Talk "suggests the hollow tones of officialese" (ix). Gibson goes on to say that traces of each of these styles appear in everything that we write, depending upon how, as writers, we want to present ourselves to our readers. To assist us in identifying each of these styles, Gibson sets up a category scheme, with subjective pronouns being the most significant determiner of style type. The Tough Talker uses first person pronouns because he focuses on himself, so Gibson refers to this prose style as "I-talk." The Sweet Talker talks directly to us, wants us to feel as if we are being well treated; this is "you-talk." The Stuffy Talker, last of all, expresses little interest in himself or in others; this style is "it-talk" says Gibson (x).

Students can have fun with Gibson's scheme in a number of ways. Before introducing them to the scheme, you can give them three short pieces of prose written in these distinctly different styles (Gibson provides numerous examples in Tough, Sweet, and Stuffy). Have the students determine what characteristics make the three pieces different from one another. Having used this inductive approach, provide the students with a sample of "The Style Machine."

One of the bonuses of using this scheme is to teach students the variety of voices that exist within themselves. For example, students also can have fun imitating each of these styles with their own work. Have them rewrite a paragraph or two of their own writing in each of these three styles, read them in small groups, and hear the different voices that emerge from each one of them.

To show your students a sample of Sweet Talk, you can use most any advertisement. Below are examples of Tough Talk and Stuffy Talk that Gibson presents in his book.

**Tough Talk**
We shall go on to the end, we shall fight in France, we shall fight on the seas and oceans, we shall fight with growing confidence and growing strength in the air, we shall defend our Island, whatever the cost may be, we shall fight on the beaches, we shall fight on the landing grounds, we shall fight in the fields and in the streets, we shall fight in the hills, ; we shall never surrender, and even if, which I do not for a moment believe, this Island or a large part of it were subjugated and starving, then our Empire beyond the seas, armed, and guarded by the British fleet, would carry on the struggle, until, in God's good time, the New World, with all its power and might, steps forth to the rescue and the liberation of the old (Gibson, 143). -- from Winston Churchill

**Stuffy Talk**

Cigarette smoking is causally related to lung cancer in men; the magnitude of the effect of cigarette smoking far outweighs all other factors. The data for women, though less extensive, point in the same direction.

The risk of developing lung cancer increases with duration of smoking and the number of cigarettes smoked per day, and is diminished by discontinuing smoking.

The risk of developing cancer of the lung for the combined group of pipe smokers, cigar smokers, and pipe and cigar smokers is greater than for nonsmokers but much less than for cigarette smokers.

The data are insufficient to warrant a conclusion for each group individually (Gibson, 93).  --from The Surgeon General's Report

The chart that follows illustrates eight of the salient characteristics that distinguish each of Gibson's three styles.

---

THE STYLE MACHINE: Criteria for Measuring Style[2]

|  | Tough | Sweet | Stuffy |
|---|---|---|---|
| One syllable words | 70%+ | 61-70% | 60% or less |
| Words of 3+ syllables | <10% | 10-19% | >20% |
| 1st and 2nd Person Pronouns | 1% "I" or "we"1st and 2nd person pronouns | 2% "you" | 0% either |
| Subjects: neuter vs. people | 50%+ people | 50%+ people | 66%+ neuter |

| Passive verbs | less than 1 in 20 | none | more than 1 in 5 |
|---|---|---|---|
| Average length of clauses | 10 words or less | 10 words or less | more than 10 words |
| Contractions & fragments | 1+ per 100 words | 2 or more | none |
| Parentheses, etc. | none | 2+ per 100 words | none |

---

## PROOFREADING

Proofreading differs from editing in that a writer is not making significant changes in the text at this point. Proofreading is a last read over for grammatical errors, spelling errors, punctuation errors, and so on.

In fact, I have students proofread one last time as they are preparing to turn in their papers. At the beginning of class, on the day that the paper is due, I give them ten to fifteen minutes to read over their papers one last time. I tell them to use their pens and to make very neatly any corrections that they want to at that time.

Like all other stages of writing, guiding students through the proofreading stage during classtime emphasizes the importance of taking a last look at the finished product. Just as the painter looks one last time at the wall and adds a dab of paint here and there, so the writer looks one last time and adds a comma here and there, deletes a word, and corrects a misspelled word to ensure that the paper is exactly as he or she intended it to be.

This chapter has introduced a wide variety of intervention kinds of work that you can engage your students in at the editing stage of their writing. These examples only begin to identify some of the possibilities. Once you use one activity, you'll have numerous ideas of your own. These are intended only to be springboards to your own imagination and to your own students' needs.

WORKS CITED Chapter 9

Christensen, Francis. "A Generative Rhetoric of the Sentence." Rhetoric and Composition: A Sourcebook for Teachers. Ed. Richard L. Graves. Rochelle Park, New Jersey: Hayden Book Company, Inc, 1976. 129-138.

Cooper, Charles R. "An Outline for Writing Sentence-Combining Problems." Rhetoric and Composition: A Sourcebook for Teachers. Ed. Richard L. Graves. Rochelle Park, New Jersey: Hayden Book Company, Inc, 1976. 118-128.

Danielewicz, Jane, and Wallace Chafe. "How 'Normal' Speaking Leads to 'Erroneous' Punctuating." The Acquisition of Written Language: Response and Revision. Ed. Sarah Warshauer Freedman. Norwood, New Jersey: Ablex Publishing Corporation, 1985. 213-225.

Gibson, Walker. Tough, Sweet, and Stuffy. Bloomington, Indiana: Indiana University Press, 1966.

Graser, Elsa R. Teaching Writing: A Process Approach. Dubuque, Iowa: Kendall/Hunt Publishing Company, 1983.

Odell, Lee. "Measuring Changes in Intellectual Processes as One Dimension of Growth in Writing." Evaluating Writing: Describing, Measuring, Judging. Eds. Charles R. Cooper and Lee Odell. Urbana, Illinois: National Council of Teachers of English, 1977.

Shaughnessy, Mina P. Errors and Expectations: A Guide for the Teacher of Basic Writing. New York: Oxford University Press, 1977.

Strong, William. Sentence Combining: A Composing Book. New York: Random House, Inc., 1973.

Winterowd, W. Ross. Contemporary Rhetoric: A Conceptual Background with Readings. New York: Harcourt, Brace, Jovanovich, Inc., 1975.

## FOOT NOTES

[1] The useful classroom applications of Odell's system were introduced to me by Terry Mosher of the State University of New York College at Fredonia.

[2] From Walker Gibson, Tough, Sweet, and Stuffy, p. 136.

# CHAPTER 10:
# EVALUATION: THE FINAL STAGE

At last you've gotten to the final stage in your students' writing: it's time to evaluate what they have written. Odell suggests that when we evaluate our students' writing, whatever system we use, we should be answering these questions: "How well are students doing? What do they need to do to become better writers" (Defining 96). You may have been answering these questions and evaluating students' writing on an ongoing basis if you have had conferences, read rough drafts, and had students review one another's work.

The stage of evaluation that this chapter talks about has to do with choosing the appropriate system of evaluating the finished piece of writing, making comments on students papers, and giving grades. This is usually the last stage in a student's written work. However, if you wish, you can allow or request students to revise their papers again; or, you can use a system of grading known as "portfolio grading" and grade a significant portion of their work again at the end of the semester.

Evaluating your students' writing comes with some important issues to consider. For one thing, evaluating writing is unlike evaluating almost anything else because the evaluation itself is an integral part of writing and its teaching. Irmscher says that "Evaluating an essay cannot be reduced to mathematical averaging, but it can become a process in which various elements of the writing are considered" (155). Thus, your evaluation of students' writing should guide them in improving their writing, unlike evaluation in other subject areas where the evaluation shows students what knowledge they have mastered. Through your evaluation of their writing, the students should learn about the strengths and weaknesses of their own writing; they should feel good about what they do well, and they should feel as if they can learn what they don't do particularly well. In other words, students should find their evaluation a positive learning experience.

Since you will give a variety of kinds of writing assignments-- journals, in-class (on-the-spot) timed writing, long-term foraml writing projects--you'll want to know a variety of kinds of evaluation methods. Each of the evaluation methods that is discussed in this chapter is suitable for some kinds of writing assignments, but not all. Thus, we need to vary our evaluation methods to suit the writing task, and most importantly, we must let students know HOW they will be evaluated.

The rest of this chapter describes the following aspects of evaluating your students' writing:

- criteria for good writing
- grades on student writing
- systems for evaluating writing
- commenting on student writing

## CRITERIA FOR GOOD WRITING

What do you look for when you evaluate your students' writing? How do you know what constitutes "good writing"? Most of us intuitively know what a piece of good writing looks like, but faced with a student who says, "Why was this a good paper?" we need to have some foundation from which to respond.

Defining and describing what you value in a piece of writing make your criteria as objective as possible. Letting your students know ahead of time what you will value in a particular assignment is extremely important for them in their attempts to be successful with their writing for your class. What makes one student's paper more successful than another's? Depending on your assignment and the emphasis that you are giving to particular features, the following criteria (adapted from Measure for Measure: A Guidebook for Evaluating Students' Expository Writing, page 3) signal good writing:

Content
- The paper is focused on a particular subject.
- The purpose of the paper is clear to its readers.
- The generalization (thesis) is well supported.
- There are adequate details to support each of the writer's points.

Organization
- The introduction gets the reader's attention and prepares the reader for what's coming.
- The organization is easy to follow.
- There is a clear transition from one idea to the next.
- Individual paragraphs are coherent.
- All details develop the purpose of the paper.
- the conclusion draws the paper to a close, summarizes the main points, and reemphasizes the paper's purpose.

Style
- Sentences reflect a variety of syntactic structures.
- Lexical choices (vocabulary) reflect a concern for the audience for and the purpose of the paper.

Correctness
- Mechanics are correct--accurate punctuation, capitalization, spelling, and grammar.
- Words are used accurately.
- Sentences are complete and correct--no comma splices, fragments, run-ons.

The above criteria are general kinds of features that all good writing has in common. Each of your writing assignments will also have specific features that you will look for. For example, if your students write a paper for the purpose of giving instructions, you'll want to give special emphasis to the order of the steps and the inclusion of some precautions. You might find that, after you have introduced a particular technique, such as "showing writing," you will want to emphasize elaboration in the assignment for that unit. Let your students know what you will be looking for in particular, and how you will weight individual features of their writing for each assignment.

## GRADES FOR STUDENT WRITING

Once you have identified the basic criteria for good writing, the next question to ask yourself is this: How do you know what constitutes a specific grade, i.e., an "A," a "B," a "C," a "D," and an "F"? Or in some cases, how do you know what the difference between a "PASS" and a "FAIL" grade is?

Unlike grading in other academic courses, in a writing course, if you can prolong giving grades, you probably should. Since most freshman students come to us fairly grade conscious, it's good to try to move them beyond thinking about their grades in your course to thinking about working on and improving their writing. Most important at the beginning of the semester is building a working relationship with each of them. Perhaps the best way to do this is to avoid grading the early work in favor of giving the students only your comments about their writing. In this way, you can emphasize what they know, praising their accomplishments, not pointing out all their errors, which could make them think that the road ahead of them for the semester is a long one.

With these recommendations aside, you will at some point need to grade your students work. One thing to think about is where to begin with your students' writing. Do you assume that every student is a "C" student, an average student who then moves up or down the grade ladder? Do your students all enter with an "A" in your mind, and then they fall from that point? Do they all begin with an "F"? The philosophical stance in these questions is an important one: if students begin at the "C" point, you may find yourself hesitating to give an "A"; if they begin at the "F" point, the climb ahead looks long and slow indeed, and again you might find yourself hesitant to give high grades; if students enter with an "A," they have no where to go but down.

Another point of reference, one that students need to know and understand, has to do with your categories. If a "C" is representative of the average, students need to know what "average" looks like and what they would have to do to move from the "C" in either direction. This is a good place to show them a sample essay, your grading criteria, and together evaluate the essay.

As teachers, we need to be careful of what Irmscher calls "eccentricity of judgment" (155) in our grading. "Eccentricity of judgment occurs when an instructor ignores completely one or more of the elements we have defined in the makeup of writing:" the content, the organization, the style, the correctness (155). Some instructors grade on content almost exclusively, while others (though very few) grade on mechanics almost entirely. While the emphasis certainly is not on mechanics in current composition pedagogy, neither of these elements should be favored to the exclusion of the other in the grading process. While many instructors do weigh content, organization, and style more heavily than mechanics, students should understand the grading system before it is implemented. If time permits, this is a good place to give the students a number of essays to look at and evaluate themselves, using your grading criteria.

The following grading criteria was adapted from Roger Garrison's book How A Writer Works. It suggests the differences among the five possible grades (A-F) based on the criteria discussed earlier:

An "A" essay --

- CONTENT: The writing is packed with information. There is a clear central idea supported by concrete details that are relevant. There is a "perfect" feeling to the essay.

- ORGANIZATION: Essay proceeds smoothly and logically from point to point, and so the essay is easy to read. Individual paragraphs are unified, coherent, and logical.

- STYLE: Writer's persona comes through immediately and clearly. Sentences have effective variety. Word choice is excellent--accurate, concrete, sensitive vocabulary.

- CORRECTNESS: There are few mechanical errors (grammar, spelling, punctuation) and none of them could cause a misreading of the message.

A "B" essay ---

Has most of the characteristics of an "A" paper, BUT:

- CONTENT: Information is not as plentiful as in the "A" essay. Supporting details generally good and relevant but may occasionally be thin.

- ORGANIZATION: Information is clearly organized, and reader does not have trouble discerning meaning. Individual paragraphs overall are unified and coherent.

- STYLE: Sentences occasionally need to be clearer, less awkward. Word choices are clear and concrete for the most part, creating an effective voice but sometimes inconsistent voice.

- CORRECTNESS: Punctuation is usually correct; few mechanical errors, but these do not cause a misreading of the message.

A "C" essay ---

- CONTENT: Central idea needs to be more specific, not frivolous or shallow. Uses too much general supporting information that may be repetitious or unnecessary; needs more specifics.

- ORGANIZATION: Sometimes not clear; reader may need to reread to ascertain meaning. Paragraphs are not always unified or tend to stray from the main point slightly. Transitions are not always clear or present.

- STYLE: Sentences need more variety. Phrases are often misplaced. Writing is often vague and unclear, characterized by ambiguous words and/or phrases and cliches.

- CORRECTNESS: Several grammatical, spelling, and punctuation errors, sometimes causing misreading of the message.

A "D" essay ---

- CONTENT: Central idea is not clear. May not have enough supporting information--facts, details, or specifics. The reader does not always get a clear picture of the writer's message. Often includes irrelevant, repetitious, unnecessary information.

- ORGANIZATION: The paper has problems with logic. Reader has to reread to understand the writer's order. Paragraphs are usually not unified and coherent. Transitions are not effective or not present.

- STYLE: Sentences have little or no variety. Word choices are unclear or inappropriate for the audience.

- CORRECTNESS: Many grammatical errors which often interfere with the message.

An "F" essay ---

- CONTENT: The essay has no central idea. The supporting information is irrelevant, unnecessary, and/or inaccurate.

- ORGANIZATION: Overall organization is unclear making the writer's purpose impossible to discern. Paragraphs are not unified or coherent and lack transitions.

- STYLE: Sentences are short and unvaried, sometimes incomplete. Sentences often seem immature and boring. Word choice is inappropriate.

- CORRECTNESS: Message is blurred by frequent errors in grammar, punctuation, and spelling. Sloppy visual presentation.

Irmscher makes a point of elaborating what most instructors feel: the "B" grade is the hardest to determine. He says,

> The clearest difference between the C-writer and the B-writer is that the B-writer seems to be in control of the writing. It doesn't just happen. It has purpose, direction, and strategy. The clearest difference between the B-writer and the A-writer is that the A-writer often brings intellectual and imaginative resources to the task of writing that transforms the material and language in some unusual way. That quality comes through clearly (156-7).

SYSTEMS OF EVALUATION

Depending on the type of writing tasks you have had your students do, you'll want to choose one of the systems for evaluating their papers that is described next: holistic scoring, analytical scales, dichotomous scales, primary trait scoring, portfolio grading, and traditional grading--commenting on student papers.

## HOLISTIC SCORING

Holistic scoring answers the question, "How well does this piece of writing work as a whole?" A grading procedure for reading and ranking pieces of student writing impressionistically, holistic evaluation assumes that the writing can and should be read as a whole, not as separate parts. Thus, the tone, the content, the organization, the purpose and audience converge to create a message that communicates as a whole. As Cooper says, "a piece of writing communicates a whole message with a particular tone to a known audience for some purpose: information, argument, amusement, ridicule, titillation" (3). Therefore, the piece of writing can be scored as a whole, or holistically.

Holistic grading is most often used when there are lots of essays to be read for placement purposes, for exiting courses, for graduation, for pre- and post-test comparison. If your college has what is commonly called "panel grading" of an exit exam, this is the type of grading that will be used.

In the context of your classroom, holistic evaluation is useful with shorter pieces of writing. For example, if you have students write in class, under pressure and time constraints, holistic grading is a good way to evaluate writing of this type.

You can also use this type of holistic reading and rating with your students, as Najimy suggests. Ask the students to write a short piece in class. Have them identify themselves by number or some pseudonym so that they can remain anonymous. Divide the class into groups of three or four and distribute their papers among these groups of students, being careful not to get a students' paper in the evaluating group of which he or she is a member. Have the groups read each of the pieces and score them holistically on a scale of 1- 4 (with 4 being excellent). For the next class, duplicate some of the papers for class discussion of the content, organization, style, and correctness. This kind of exercise leads to students' better understanding of good writing. It is also a useful activity to engage students in before they revise their own longer papers. This activity should take no more than a total of fifty minutes (7-8).

## ANALYTICAL SCALES

Describing an analytical scale, Cooper says that "an analytic scale is a list of the prominent features or characteristics of writing in a particular mode" (7). The following scale is a well known one developed by Diederich (1974) to evaluate college freshman writing (reproduced in Cooper, 7):

| General merit | Low | | Middle | | High | |
|---|---|---|---|---|---|---|
| Ideas | 2 | 4 | 6 | 8 | 10 | |
| Organization | 2 | 4 | 6 | 8 | 10 | |
| Wording | 1 | 2 | 3 | 4 | 5 | |
| Flavor | 1 | 2 | 3 | 4 | 5 | ____ |
| Mechanics | | | | | | |
| Usage | 1 | 2 | 3 | 4 | 5 | |
| Punctuation | 1 | 2 | 3 | 4 | 5 | |
| Spelling | 1 | 2 | 3 | 4 | 5 | |
| Handwriting | 1 | 2 | 3 | 4 | 5 | ____ |

Total ____

To use this analytical scale, you would give a student's paper points in each category, multiply the result by two, and give the student a numerical score for his or her essay.

## DICHOTOMOUS SCALES

Another grading system is known as a "dichotomous scale." The dichotomous scale is a series of descriptions of features that should appear in a piece of good writing. The rater simply decides if the piece has the feature (e.g., Insightful ideas) or not.

## PRIMARY TRAIT SCORING

Primary Trait Scoring is a scoring method that can be very useful in your own grading. Developed by Lloyd-Jones (1974) for the National Assessment of Educational Progress, Primary Trait Scoring directs the reader's attention to specific features of a particular kind of discourse: "to the special blend of audience, speaker role, purpose, and subject required by that kind of discourse and by the particular writing task" (Cooper, 11). For example, if the students were writing a persuasive letter about a campus problem, one of the features of this task would be form. Scorers, using the Primary Trait Scoring method, would look at the students' letters and judge the form of the letter as one part of the process since letter form would be a primary criteria. Another criteria could be the kinds of persuasive appeals that the students use. Each of the traits is scored on a scale that is established before the grading takes place; that is, each trait is assigned a range of possible points.  Thus, the trait "letter form" might be assigned a range of 0-2 points (0=not in letter form; 1=letter form but is missing one or more of the standard parts; 2=good letter form).

Lloyd-Jones claims that Primary Trait Scoring does not assume, as do other forms of holistic scoring, that excellence in one mode predicts excellence in others.  For example, a student might write an outstanding description of her grandmother's 100th birthday, but be less adequate at writing a persuasive letter asking to be readmitted to a college.  Lloyd-Jones says that "The goal of Primary Trait Scoring is to define precisely what segment of discourse will be evaluated . . . and to train readers to render holistic judgments accordingly" (37).

While this system was devised to grade large numbers of essays for placement purposes, it is a system that you can adapt for use in your own grading, too.  For example, I usually provide my students with comment sheets, which are dittoed descriptions of my grading criteria.  I give these to the students a class or two before they are due to hand in their final papers and write comments on the sheets when I return the students' papers to them.

On these comment sheets, I break down the grading into the major categories of "content," "organization," "style," and "correctness." Under each of these categories I describe what I am looking for in terms of each category for the specific assignment the students are about to turn in.  In this way, I can tailor my expectations to each particular assignment since for example, the organization of a persuasive paper might draw more attention than that of an expressive one.  This procedure synthesizes a traditional grading system with the Primary Trait Scoring method in a way that gives students specific information about particular assignments.

## PORTFOLIO GRADING

Portfolio grading has become an interesting alternative to traditional grading in writing classes.  It combines conferencing, workshopping, and multiple drafting in a system that deemphasizes grades and grading.

Portfolio grading works in a composition class much like portfolios work for artists, as a representation of what the student has done over a period of time.  A student works on a number of essays over the course of the semester, selects a few to polish up near the end of the semester, and turns in a portfolio of his or her selected work at the end of the semester for grading.  This system has a number of advantages for both the student and the teacher. The issue of grading is placed squarely on the student's shoulders since they select the pieces that the instructor will evaluate; in the system of portfolio grading that is described later, students also decide whether to "compete" for a grade above a "C." The system also allows for multiple revisions throughout the semester, giving students the opportunity to implement the skills that they have learned throughout the semester. The teacher takes on the role of respondent, rather than judge, for most of the semester. Students work a lot with one another on reading and making recommendations for revision. Last, the student selects what he or she determines to be the best work from a larger number of essays.

The system has some disadvantages, too. Since students are quite grade conscious, you need to make provisions for giving students interim grades if they insist. If you are not careful, you can become more a director of the students' revisions than a reader and responder. At the end of the semester, you have a lot of reading to do, but since you have already read drafts of the essays and have talked about them in conference with the students, this should be less demanding than it might appear at the onset.

Burnham (1986) itemizes some possible criteria for the Portfolio Evaluation system that has been designed and implemented at New Mexico State University, and described in "Portfolio Evaluation: Room to Breathe and Grow."

1.  PORTFOLIO OVERVIEW: At specified times during the semester, students submit finished drafts of essays that they have been working on. Instructors respond to these, giving suggestions for revisions, but do not give the papers a grade. When the instructor decides that the student has met the assignment's minimum requirements, the instructor accepts the assignment as finished. The student can go on to the next assignment in the sequence for the semester.

2.  GRADING: After completing the specified number of assignments (at New Mexico State University the students are assigned nine and must successfully complete seven), the students can choose to put together a portfolio for final evaluation. If they do not want to compile the portfolio, and they have completed all the assignments successfully, they get a "C" for the course. By compiling a portfolio, they are competing for a higher grade, though this is not a guarantee.

At NMSU, the portfolio includes samples of all of the students' best writing: freewriting, journal writing, narratives, poems, etc. It also includes two essays that were previously submitted and considered finished, but for the portfolio have been revised substantially. The student turns in both the previous drafts and the revised version.

Last, the students write explanations of what makes the writing good that has been included in the portfolio and a persuasive paper defending the grade they believe they have earned.

3.  CONFERENCING: As the instructor using the portfolio system, you need to conference regularly with the students.   Three conferences are essential to the NMSU method.  During a midterm conference, the instructor lets students know how they are progressing in the course.  It is also a time to "shake students out of their complacency and drive them toward realizing their potential" (132).  Thus, students who need a little prodding, get it in time to turn their work around.  This is also a time to give provisional grades if students really want them, and a time when students can still drop the class if they are doing poorly.  The second conference at NMSU is a clearance interview about four weeks before the end of the semester.   This is the final preparation for compiling portfolios.  During this conference, you can discuss the criteria for getting higher grades and if that is feasible for a given student; also make certain that students understand the system (e.g., submitting a portfolio does not immediately guarantee an "A" or a "B."). During the final interview, you discuss the students' portfolio and final grade for the course--whether the student received the grade that he or she requested; a single strength in writing that the student should continue to develop and one or two areas the student still needs to work on.  Besides these three conferences, you'll want to conference regularly over the students papers, and you'll want to have frequent in-class writing workshops (125-38).

As Burnham states, "The procedure, portfolio evaluation, incorporates what we know about how students develop as writers by emphasizing process, multiple drafting, and collaborative learning.  In addition, portfolio evaluation encourages instructors to become respondents to student writing rather than error-seeking proofreaders" (126).

## TRADITIONAL GRADING: COMMENTING ON STUDENTS' PAPERS

I've saved this system for last in this chapter because it is the most frequently used system and because it, in many ways, can synthesize the best of the systems discussed so far in this section of the chapter.

In traditional grading, instructors often incorporate bits and pieces of the other systems. For example, an instructor might provide students with a grading sheet that includes a dichotomous scale, identifying what features were present or not. This is especially useful for the mechanical elements of a text. The grading sheet also might include the kind of Primary Trait Scoring that I mentioned in the previous section. Essentially, however, the traditional system of grading involves three main ingredients: suggested surface changes, marginal comments, and terminal comments. Before talking about these individually, I'm going to give you a few comments about how we encounter student texts as readers, interpreting students' texts.


## READING STUDENT TEXTS

Reading our students' texts is a process of interpretation not much different from reading a piece of literature or a letter from a friend. As we read, we need to remember all of the potential influences that have contributed to making the texts that are in front of us, and, as a result, that there is probably not one absolute way to interpret what a student is meaning to say.

In Encountering Student Texts, Lawson, Ryan, and Winterowd remind us "that it is naive to talk about a 'correct way' to read a student essay. Student texts, like literary works, are complex and slippery things, and we must be intensely self-conscious as interpreters. Just as our literature classes are enlivened by multiple approaches to the texts, so our encounters with student writing may become more productive as we consider alternative ways of interpreting and responding to those dauntingly alive, complex and troubling creations our students hand us at the end of class sessions" (2-3). Thus, we need to remind ourselves of the myriad of influences that come to bear on student writing, their academic, social, political, personal lives all contribute to the writing that we receive. This observation is not meant to turn you into a "dime-store" psychologist, only to remind you that written products are much more than meets the eye, and we should keep this in the back of our minds as we read and comment upon our students' texts.

In addition, it is probably also useful to keep in the back of our minds the assumptions that Odell suggests influence our reading of texts. One assumption is that our knowledge is contingent and uncertain, "constrained by the perspectives from which we examine any body of information. Our process of observing or reading is not simply a passive recording of what is 'out there,' but, rather, is a complex interpretive process that is profoundly influenced by our values, needs, past experiences, and even, as Stanley Fish (1980) has pointed out, out membership in a particular social group" (224). Thus, as readers and evaluators, we too, bring assumptions to the texts that our students have written. The second assumption that Odell identifies is that "the process of writing is often a social process . . . identifying and trying to accommodate the needs and interests of the person or group of people that comprise a writer's audience" (224). Having targeted their audience as best they can, our student writers then hope that their texts are understood in the way that they intended for them to be. As responders this advice adds up to remembering that "texts do not evolve in a vacuum" (Odell, 224). Neither should our comments to our students.

Unlike in a math class where the answer is right or wrong, students' papers (or answers to our assignments) fall into a continuum of right responses. When we pass papers back to the students who wrote them, and the papers have comments from us to the students, it's important that our comments to the students strike a positive and encouraging note. If we want students to work hard at something as personal as writing, we need to motivate them. Our comments have the power to do that.


SUGGESTING SURFACE CHANGES


Surface changes include such features as word choice, punctuation correction, grammatical corrections, and other mechanical changes. The rule of thumb with these is this: do not mark all of the students' errors. Resist the temptation to think that you have not done your job if you have left some errors unmarked. There are a number of ways to handle surface comments.

Concentrate your marks on one or two fairly prevalent errors which could continue to be problems in the student's writing. If you do this, refer the student to the appropriate section of the textbook or handbook that you are using for help in understanding the errors. If there are many different kinds of errors, select one or two to work on as a starting point.  Remember that most students cannot work on all these grammatical and mechanical principles at one time.  They will likely feel defeated if the paper that is returned is covered by corrections on the surface level.

Some people correct only a portion of the essay, for example, just the first page.  If you do this, correct a variety of errors on the first page, and tell the student that these are representative of the kinds of errors that occur elsewhere in the paper.  You could have students look for and correct their own errors based on the corrections that you have made in this segment of the text.

The "error log" (Boley, 1989) is another approach to working students through their own errors.  Place a check mark in the margin opposite a line where an error occurs.  To complete an error log, the student must locate the error, identify it by referring to the handbook you are using, record it a section of his notebook called the Error Log and reserved for this purpose, correct the error, and explain the rule.  This is time consuming for both you and the student, but it is an effective way to teach students about mechanics through their own writing.

Whichever system you choose for pointing out some of the students' surface errors, with some practice you'll begin to feel easier about not marking every one of the student's mistakes.

## MARGINAL COMMENTS

Comments written in the side margins of students' papers are one of the most useful kinds of comments you make on students' papers.  When you write comments in the margin, be sure to include praise about what the student has done well or effectively.  Praising gives your comments the instructive power that you want them to have since it balances out the constructive criticism that you'll also offer. Besides, you want the students to continue to do well what they've done well.

Your constructive criticism--the things you want student to work on for next time--in your marginal comments shouldn't simply label problems, but they should explain how, where, why the writing suffers.  Questions requiring real thought, ones that can't be answered with a word or two, get the student to reread what he has written and to reconsider its effectiveness.  For example, a question in the margin can get the student to rethink and recast some description to make the writing come alive.  A question such as "What was this raft ride down the Colorado River like?   Can you describe your feelings and your responses to that ride so your reader will experience it with you?" will do this.

The following recommendations about marginal comments are adapted from Larson (1986, 113-14):

1.   Refer to something specific, either a strength or a weakness.

2.   Ask questions that point out where something needs clarified or where other views of the subject could be considered, always being sure to let the student know that you are interested in what he or she has to say.

3.   Avoid ambiguous markings, such as a "?" without any comment, a "So what?" or a "Huh?" These kinds of comments can be confusing to the student and just leave him guessing about what you really mean.

4.   For the most part, don't argue with the student.  Allow him or her a point of view, even one you might disagree with, as long as it is developed logically.

5.   Be sure to note where the student's style, organization, content, or thinking is good.  A "well stated" can do wonders for the student's ego, and consequently, for the student's motivation.

## TERMINAL COMMENTS

Unlike marginal comments that speak to specific points in the students' papers, terminal comments are general comments that appear at the very end of the paper and sum up, in general, what you have to say about the paper as a whole.  When you make a terminal comment, think about your impressions of the paper as a whole: how well the student responded to the assignment and how effectively communicated, for example.  Marginal comments and the terminal comments should support one another.   As Larson (1986) says, "the two sets of observations should work together.  . . . [T]he general comment should not be merely a disjointed summary or repetition of the marginal comments.  It must bring your separate responses to the paper into focus; it must give the student a coherent assessment of the paper as a whole" (116).

The following recommendations about terminal comments are adapted from Larson (1986, 114-16):

1. Point out the paper's strengths and its good points; don't concentrate solely on its weaknesses and aspects that need to be improved upon.

2. Maintain the student's ownership of the paper. Often, it is easy to look at a paper as something done for us when really we want student to look at their papers as their own. Try to see the paper from the student's perspective as much as possible.

3. Describe how well the student addressed the assignment overall.

4. Concentrate on overall issues of content, organization, and style that affect the paper as a whole. Propose and explain changes that you recommend so that the student can see clearly what the difficulty was and how to go about revising to improve the paper. Whether or not you have students revise their papers after this evaluation, the terminal comment should help the students with future assignments.

5. Use language that will be clear to the student. That means to avoid flip or sarcastic comments. Sometimes a student will understand these, but more often than not, they will be hurt or angered by a flip, sarcastic, or ironic tone. Remember to view these comments as one more opportunity to instruct your students on a on-to-one basis. Along the same lines, focus the comments on the paper and the writing, not on the student's motivation for writing the paper or on his or her personality.

Depending on the number of students you have and the length of their papers, commenting on student papers can be time consuming. With practice, it begins to move more quickly. Reviewing students' earlier drafts also makes the final evaluation process go more quickly. Also, keep in mind that you can't comment on everything about the paper, nor should you even try. Be focused on the students' responses to the specific assignment and how that matches up to your goals for the assignment. Last, remember those one or two particular features of each student's writing at which you're looking.

Having completed the evaluation of your students' papers, you have finished one complete cycle in teaching writing. Now, it's time for the cycle to begin all over again. Congratulations and good luck!

WORKS CITED Chapter 10

Boley, Tommy. "The Error Log." University of Texas at El Paso: El Paso, Texas, 1989.

Burnham, Christopher C. "Portfolio Evaluation: Room to Breathe and Grow." Training the New Teacher of College Composition. Ed. Charles W. Bridges. Urbana, Illinois: National Council of Teachers of English, 1986.

Cooper, Charles R. "Holistic Evaluation of Writing." Evaluating Writing: Describing, Measuring, Judging. Eds. Charles R. Cooper and Lee Odell. Urbana, Illinois: National Council of Teachers of English, 1977.

Garrison, Roger. How A Writer Works. Rev. ed. New York: Harper & Row Publishers, 1985.

Irmscher, William F. Teaching Expository Writing. New York: Holt, Rinehart and Winston, 1979.

Larson, Richard L. "Making Assignments, Judging Writing, and Annotating Papers: Some Suggestions." Training the New Teacher of College Composition. Ed. Charles W. Bridges. Urbana, Illinois: National Council of Teachers of English, 1986.

Lawson, Bruce, Susan Sterr Ryan, and W. Ross Winterowd, eds. Encountering Student Texts: Interpretive Issues in Reading Student Writing. Eds. Bruce Lawson, Susan Sterr Ryan, and W. Ross Winterowd. Urbana, Illinois: National Council of Teachers of English, 1990

Lloyd-Jones, Richard. "Primary Trait Scoring." Evaluating Writing: Describing, Measuring, Judging. Eds. Charles R. Cooper and Lee Odell. Urbana, Illinois: National Council of Teachers of English, 1977.

Najimy, Norman, C., ed. Measure for Measure: A Guidebook for Evaluating Students' Expository Writing. Urbana, Illinois: National Council of Teachers of English, 1981.

Odell, Lee. "Defining and Assessing Competence in Writing." The Nature and Measure of Competency in English. Ed. Charles R. Cooper. Urbana, Illinois: National Council of Teachers of English, 1981. 95-138.

---. "Responding to Responses: Good News, Bad News, and Unanswered Questions." <u>Encountering Student Texts: Interpretive Issues in Reading Student Writing</u>. Eds. Bruce Lawson, Susan Sterr Ryan, and W. Ross Winterowd. Urbana, Illinois: National Council of Teachers of English, 1990. 221-234.